TOMMY TAYLOR
of
MANCHESTER UNITED and BARNSLEY

'A Busby Babe'

An illustrated Biography
By John Kennedy

Published by:
Yore Publications
12 The Furrows, Harefield,
Middx. UB9 6AT.

© John Kennedy 1994

....

British Library Cataloguing-in-Publication Data.
A catalogue record for this book
is available from the British Library.

ISBN 1 874427 85 2

(The majority of the photographs in this book were supplied by the friends and relations of Tommy Taylor. For the few exceptions, every effort has been made to trace the source in order to ensure that copyright has not been infringed)

Yore Publications specialise in football books, normally of an historic theme. Newsletters (which detail all current and new titles) are posted free, three times per year. Please send a S.A.E. for your initial copy of the latest Newsletter.

Printed by 'The Book Factory'

ACKNOWLEDGEMENTS

Harry, Irene, Wayne, Mathew and Paul England. Bill, Audrey and Ian Taylor. Irene and Jim Kossowicz. Alice Powell. Peter Taylor. The late Thomas Taylor. Elliot Taylor. Doug Kelly. Norma Webster. Harold Hackney. Bob McCormick. Johnny Steele. Andrew and Keith Lodge. Albert Scanlon. Johnny Carey. Allenby Chilton. Henry Cockburn. Harry Gregg. Ray Wood. Jeff Whitefoot. Sir Walter Winterbottom. Ian Greaves. Tom Finney. The late Billy Wright. Frank Taylor. Ron Church. Bob Beard. Iain McCartney. Ray Adler. Angela Ray at Pottersbury Secretarial Services. Steve White at Archway Photographic.

Special thanks to Barnsley F.C. Club Historian Arthur Bower whose assistance was to prove so valuable.

And finally my wife Christine and children Chantelle, Danielle and Hannah for their patience and encouragement these last 2 years.

This book is dedicated to Harry England

CONTENTS

'The Boy From Smithies'

Foreword

By Harry Gregg

Being asked by John Kennedy to write the foreword for his book on the late great Tommy Taylor causes me some sadness, however, it also gives me great pleasure. Can I say, most of all, I consider it an honour.

I was fortunate enough to play not only with Tommy at Manchester United, but against him at International level (Tommy for England, myself for Northern Ireland). In my opinion, the greatest football era was the fifties and sixties. At that period of time I was fortunate enough to play against the Worlds greatest forwards, and I can honestly say that Tommy at 26 years of age was ranked with the best of them. Sadly, but for the disaster, Tommy had so much more to give.

Tall and powerful, his heading ability was second to none, yet all those years ago Tommy was not the run of the mill English League centre-forward who basically played directly through the middle, (in modern football jargon) Tommy was very 'mobile', in other words, Tommy was always available right across the forward line. As the Bobby Charltons', Dennis Viollets', David Peggs', Eddie Colmans', and Duncan Edwards' would say, "Just play the ball up front, we will get it off The Big Man."

Words are cheap. Not only was Tommy Taylor a great player on the pitch, off it he was a quiet, unassuming, proud Yorkshire man, always happier out of the spotlight than in it.

My fondest, and sadly, last memory of Tommy was at the after match banquet in Belgrade. It was almost midnight, everyone was happy we had won. The final act was Mark Jones, David Pegg and Tommy Taylor leading everyone (Yugoslavs as well) in a great rendering of the Yorkshire anthem 'On Ilkley Moor Ba Tat'.

THANKS FOR
THE MEMORY

AN INTRODUCTION

I have never really been able to explain my affection for the pre-Munich Manchester United side. Although I follow the fortunes of the current team, my heart lies with the players who boarded that fateful Elizabethan aircraft on that snow-covered Munich runway in February, 1958.

Believe me, no one was more delighted when United lifted their first League crown for 26 years, but I would rather sit down and discuss the two consecutive championship wins of 1956 and 57. That's how strongly I feel for this great side.

I've always been a nostalgia buff at heart, especially where the 1950's are concerned. The music, the cars and the football were all part and parcel of my love affair for this magical decade and it is a love which has been with me ever since I was a child.

When I was younger I often heard people mention the Manchester United side of the fifties. Names such as Duncan Edwards, Roger Byrne and Tommy Taylor kept cropping up and curiosity eventually led these players to become heros of mine, although I wasn't even old enough to have seen them play. When I think about it all now, the side that perished at Munich must be rated among the greatest teams of all time.

We all have our favourite teams and from those 11 players, there is perhaps one person we admire above all the rest. It could be a goalkeeper who makes a string of match-winning saves, or a defender who times his tackles to perfection to regain possession and calmly passes the ball up field to a waiting team-mate. Or maybe it's the tall, graceful centre-forward who would run all day to aid his team-mates.... who can score goals with both feet or his head and maybe, someone who is so important to your team's success that once he is fit, he is never dropped. Tommy Taylor fits into this category with ease and that's why he's always been my favourite player. He had all the qualities needed to be a good centre-forward and these qualities made Tommy Taylor an all time great.

Matt Busby was a great player, too. In fact, in his day he was one of the finest wing-halves in the game when he played for Manchester City in the Thirties. He played for City in two consecutive FA Cup Finals. In 1933 they lost 3-0 to Everton, when the great Dixie Dean scored one of the goals. However, the following year a Frank Tilson goal three minutes from time gave City a victory over Portsmouth. The same year Busby won his only peace-time cap, against Wales, in a Home International.

He was transferred to Liverpool in 1936 for an £8,000 fee, but at the outbreak of the Second World War in September 1939, the League was suspended and Busby - on the recommendation of Sir Stanley Rous - entered the Army as a Physical Training Instructor. It was here that Matt's great leadership qualities began to develop. He eventually went on to manage the Army team where he worked with some of the greatest names in football. Players like Joe Mercer, Cliff Britton, Frank Swift, Tommy Lawton and Stanley Matthews.

Manchester United meanwhile had not had a proper Manager since Scott Duncan resigned in 1937. For some reason, a disillusioned Scott left to manage Ipswich Town, who at the time were a non-League club. Walter Crickmer, who was the clubs longest serving official, was made Secretary-Manager and his assistant, Louis Rocca, was the Chief Scout.

Rocca had come to the club in the 1890's when they were still known by their original name of *Newton Heath*. In fact Rocca often boasted that it was he who came up with the new title of Manchester United, although this is highly unlikely. However, he was responsible for the inspired signings of Tom Curry, Bill Inglis and Bert Whalley, three very respected trainers.

Rocca's masterstroke came in 1944 when he wrote to Busby asking him if he would be interested in the Manager's post at Old Trafford, and after a meeting with club Director, James Gibson, Matt Busby became United's new Manager on 19th February, 1945.

There were many outstanding players at the club at this time, and many who simply weren't good enough and had no place in the new Manager's plans. Before the outbreak of war three of United's all time greats were already at the club - Johnny Carey, Jack Rowley and finally, in 1938 (the year they were promoted back into Division One), Stan Pearson. It was these three players that were to be the backbone of Busby's first great side.

When he did take over, the future didn't look promising at all. The club had a hefty five figure overdraft and the ground at Old Trafford wasn't fit to play on due to bomb damage. In fact all home games had to be played at neighbouring Maine Road, but Busby knew the potential the club had to offer.

His first and undoubtedly greatest signing was to be Jimmy Murphy. He was most impressed with Jimmy's knowledge of the game when he heard him talking football to some troops during a training session in an Army camp in Bari, south-east Italy. Jimmy had been a hard-tackling wing-half, both for West Bromwich Albion and Wales, where he gained 22 caps. Matt explained the difficulties they would both face if he accepted the job as Assistant Manager - no money for new players and no ground. He accepted the challenge with the knowledge also that United had not won a major honour since 1911.

It was not long before some great names were gracing the football stadia up and down the country. Players such as Charlie Mitten, John Aston, Henry Cockburn, Johnny Carey and Jack Rowley were all soon to be football heroes to a new generation of soccer fans. In Matt's first season in charge, United managed a respectable fourth in the war-time Football League North.

Three years later, in 1948, United won the FA Cup in what many people describe as the finest final ever to be played at Wembley. The match versus Blackpool gave United a convincing 4-2 victory, and it gave Busby's first great side its finest hour. During this period they were runners-up in the League on three occasion, in 1947, 1948 and 1949. By 1950, however, Busby was becoming increasingly disillusioned by some of his team's performances. They were playing well, but not quite well enough.

Busby was, at this time, taking a great interest in youth. He had set up a large scouting network up and down the country, searching for talented kids who, one day, may make the grade in the rough and tumble world of the First Division. The policy of developing youth talent was not totally new at Old Trafford, for the idea of producing home-bred youngsters was first introduced by James Gibson in 1931. During a Board meeting that year Gibson spoke about, *"the advisability of running a Colts or Nursery team from next season"*. The principle laid down was that *"the job of cultivating young players must be thoroughly done to be effective."*

Between 1950 and 1952 many fresh faces began appearing at Old Trafford. Sixteen-year-old Jackie Blanchflower had arrived from Belfast. Mark Jones from Wombwell, had played for the England Schoolboys alongside another United youngster, Dennis Viollet. Jeff Whitefoot made his first team debut against Portsmouth, just as David Pegg arrived from Doncaster, and Roger Byrne - another local product - was soon to be a first team regular and Club Captain.

Manchester United were runners-up in the League in 1951, before finally winning it the following year. It was not long before the older, established players were found top jobs (such as Player/Manager) with other clubs, as more and more youngsters filtered into the side.

Not all the players were nurtured through the ranks. Ray Wood was bought in 1950 from Darlington for a £6,000 fee, and Johnny Berry for £25,000 from Birmingham City. However, the final piece of the Jigsaw came in March, 1953, with the signing of Barnsley inside-left Tommy Taylor. The story of Busby knocking £1 off the fee so as not to label him a £30,000 player is legendary.

At the time of his transfer, he was the most wanted man in English football, but the then United Chairman, Harold Hardman, thought the signing could be a gamble. This proved to be unfounded. In his first season Tommy made the first of his 19 appearances in an England shirt and he eventually went on to score 128 goals in 189 games for United. He soon became one of the most feared but most graceful centre-forwards of the era and it is generally regarded that he was the best header of the ball since Tommy's own hero, Tommy Lawton.

On 31st October, 1953, the team played Huddersfield Town in a League match which ended in a 0-0 draw. Matt Busby recalls *"October 31st 1953 was one of the most important days in the history of Manchester United and in my career as a football manager. We fielded that day in an away match with Huddersfield - who at the time were second in the table - seven youngsters of 21 or under. It was one of the youngest teams ever to take part in a First Division game. The seven were, Ray Wood, Bill Foulkes, Duncan Edwards, Jeff Whitefoot, Jackie Blanchflower, Dennis Viollet, and Tommy Taylor. After the draw with Huddersfield on heavy ground at home we were held to a 2-2 draw with Arsenal. But the next fixture away to Cardiff shattered all doubts. We went there and won 6-1."* Alf Clarke, a well respected sports writer of the time, wrote after the Huddersfield match *"Busby's bouncing babes keep Town all awake"* and from that moment on the Busby Babes legend was born.

It's always been an ambition of mine to write a book concerning the Busby Babes, but over the years there have been several excellent publications about that particular era of the Club's history, as well as two or three books on Munich. There have also been a couple of books on another United hero, Duncan Edwards. So I thought the chance of ever having anything published was virtually nil, for enough had already been written.

With the greatest respect to the other lads who died, I have always felt that besides Duncan only Tommy Taylor would warrant any kind of project. Virtually all the others came to Old Trafford as raw fifteen or sixteen year old and were groomed through youth to reserve team players to eventual appearances in the first team, but Tommy was different. He'd had five years with Barnsley and came to United with a reputation as a goalscorer. A year ago I had the chance to write something on Tommy so I took the opportunity while it was there.

I have always been a frequent visitor to the graves of the players who died in Munich - and Tommy's was no exception. When I went to Barnsley I always made sure I popped into the Athersley Arms, where I believed Tommy's best friend, Harry England, was a regular. However, he was never in while I was there, so I left my telephone number behind the bar. Two weeks went past before I received a 'phone call giving me Harry's number. After 'phoning him, I soon got an invitation to go to Barnsley so we could sit and talk about Tommy.

Harry still had a collection of mementos which Tommy had brought back from his trips abroad, as well as postcards, letters, photos etc., but the situation got even better. Harry had arranged for me to meet Tommy's only surviving brother, Bill, who suffered, like many other members of the Taylor family, a gradual move towards blindness.

I was in awe as he showed me the cabinet which housed a collection of Tommy's caps and medals and, as I sat there wearing Tommy's Cup Final strip, I suggested that I write a book as a tribute. Bill still had the scrapbooks which their mother had kept right from his days with Barnsley Boys, through to the Munich tragedy, therefore a lot of information was already to hand. So I set about my task with a boyish enthusiasm and what you are reading now is the result of all my efforts.

If you are reading this book expecting every single fact or detail to be correct, you may be disappointed. Of course I have made every effort to ensure that what I have written is accurate, but you must remember that everybody I spoke to are recollecting events that took place 40 or more years ago. So, please try not to be too critical, as I believe any new material on any of the Babes should be welcomed.

I have tried not to dwell for page after page of how this great team came into being, something I feel I have explained adequately already, or about the rise of the so called Red Devils. Even when it came to Munich I tried to go about it in a slightly different way, something that, as you can imagine, proved to be quite difficult. Whilst writing the book on Tommy, I found it quite easy to drift away from my original intention and fall into another 'Busby Babes Story' routine, so wherever possible I have tried to shed new light concerning any aspect of his career.

Tommy's exploits in the red shirt of United have been fairly well documented over the years, but not so much is known about his spells in the Army or when he played for Barnsley and Smithies Utd. For instance, how many people know he played full-back for Barnsley Boys?

To some people, some of the things in this book may seem trivial and they could ask *"Does it really matter?"* Well, it mattered to me, for I think it is quite refreshing to find out about the side of a man the crowds on the terraces or the reporters in the press box never really knew.

I hope there will be something in my book for everybody. It could be a fact you never knew or even just a photograph you have never seen before. I hope you find it interesting. Above all I hope you feel it is a fitting tribute to one of the greatest players of his generation. Tommy Taylor was a hero to many, he was an England International and was a key member of arguably the best side Manchester United ever had. For those readers who were soccer fans at the time, to those fans who are reading this now, that really says it all.

CHAPTER ONE

THE BOY FROM SMITHIES

To appreciate and understand the background in which Tommy Taylor was born and grew up, there is first a need to paint a picture of life in Yorkshire from the turn of the Century, when our story begins, through the period of two World Wars until the mid-1940s.

Tommy's family lived in Yorkshire which was - and still is today - the principal coalfield in the country. Today there are many significant differences. Most important is that in those days coal was the only major fuel in Britain and, therefore, a vital source of energy. For it was not only used in its' own right for heating the home and the workplace, but as a source of energy from which both gas and electricity were produced. It also ran all the country's railways. It was also pre-nationalisation. The National Coal Board, as it was, did not come into being until the industry was nationalised by Clement Attlee's postwar Government in 1947. Before that the industry was run by private enterprise. Being so vital to the country's needs, it was the largest employer in many parts of the country. It was a tough gruelling life for those who worked in the industry - on most occasions the only industry in their particular locality, and there was certainly no love lost between the pit owners and the men and women who worked for them.

Four members of Tommy's family appear in this photograph, which was taken outside Smithies Club around 1920. His father is at the centre of the front row, Grandad (also named 'Tommy') is on the left at the rear, in the black cap; 'Uncle Elliot' is the youngster behind him to the right, and Aunt Elizabeth is the girl in white.

There was no such thing as automation. All the coal had to be hacked out by brute force, and the industry's safety record was not like it is today. Roof collapses and explosions were all too common in those pick-and-shovel days. Methane gas, or 'firedamp' as it was known by the miners, was the killer they all feared. In those days there were some 1,400 pits employing around three-quarters of a million men. Today the industry is a mere shadow of its former self, now with some 30 coal mines employing around 40,000 people. Much of this change has come about through the mechanisation that has gradually spread throughout the industry since the 50's.

Inevitably, working in such dangerous and gruelling conditions, the miners developed a terrific sense of camaraderie and friendship together. After all, they lived together in close-knit communities, they shared the same bus to work, and they worked side-by-side either underground at or near the coal-face or in one of the surface jobs. After their shift was finished, they showered together and caught the same bus home.

When not at work, they drank at the same pubs or clubs. In most of the villages there would be a Miners' Institute, so if they did not use the pub, they would drink there instead. As in any community, their leisure pursuits were varied. Pigeon-fancying was popular and there were many artists in the making spawning art shows and competitions. Most communities had a brass band and a number spent many an hour reading in the libraries to be found in all Miners' Institutes. In the North-east growing leeks was popular and the centre for of all these activities would be the annual Miners' Gala which was a special day out for the whole family.

Football was far more of an occasion then than it is today when games can be seen without leaving the armchair. In those days it was a great opportunity to be out in the open air and share the enjoyment of a good game with your friends, whether you were taking part yourself or just a spectator.

It was a community which shared their working lives and leisure hours together. When there were disasters at the pit, the whole community would turn out and they even mourned together.......

It is against this background that the story of Tommy Taylor, who was destined to become one of the famous Busby Babes, begins. Typical of the many small mining villages in Yorkshire was Smithies. Perched on a hill overlooking the South Yorkshire town of Barnsley, it still retains much of its original character, unspoiled by multi-storey car parks and high rise housing estates. In common with the rest of the area, mining was the main source of income for the men.

Violet Hodgkis spent her early working days in the mining industry. She would either drive the pit ponies or stand for hours on end sorting out the large rocks from the coal on the conveyor belt. The work was dirty and monotonous, so when she reached the age of 17, Violet decided that enough was enough. She packed her bags and moved from her home town of Ashington. Barnsley was a nearby large town, so this was her goal. She reasoned that a larger town may give wider job opportunities outside the mines. So a move to Barnsley could lead to a brighter future. Even then, with no experience outside of mining, her prospects were going to be limited to cleaning or a job 'in service'. She hoped for a job as a cleaner or perhaps as a cleaner/chambermaid in a large house. The year was 1917.

Her search for work in Barnsley led Violet to 'Smithies Working Men's Club'. She asked to speak to the Steward who, at that time, was Thomas Taylor. All Thomas could offer her in the way of work was cleaning. It wasn't much and neither was the reward, but it was a start and one extra good thing about it was that it came with a room.

Thomas Taylor literally 'lived over the shop' at the club with all his family. There were six children in all - three daughters, Esther, Elizabeth and Ginny - and three sons - Thomas or 'Tucker' as he was known, Elliot and Charles. It was Charles who caught young Violet's eye. He was a miner at the nearby Carlton Pit and it was not long before the young couple were courting.

Football was very close to the family's heart - in fact they had a good football pedigree. Thomas senior had been a player with Barnsley when the club still went under the name of Barnsley St. Peter. Charles became a talented centre half with Wakefield City and went on to play for many local sides including Monkton Colliery, Pyewood Colliery, the Honeywell Inn and Dearne Athletic. His talents were not confined to the football pitch however, for he was also a renowned snooker and billiard player.

Charles and Violet eventually married in 1921 and moved to a house in Old Carlton Road, Smithies, moving less than a year later to 4 Quarry Street. Charles still had his job at the pit, but Violet still preferred life away from the mine itself and instead got herself a job at the Woodman Inn doing all the cleaning. It was very convenient for her as the Woodman was only a few yards away from their Quarry Street home. The landlord at the time was William Jones, although the pub was to have a closer association with the Taylor family a few years later. Charles' sister, Esther, became the landlady of the Inn, and it was not long before a football team was formed.

The couple were overjoyed when in 1922, not long after moving to Quarry Street, Violet gave birth to a son, Charles; it was always the custom in those days to name the first son after his father. However, the couples happiness was not to last. Tragedy struck early on when Charles fell down the steps which led to their front door, and as a result he developed spinal meningitis. He died when he was just three years old.

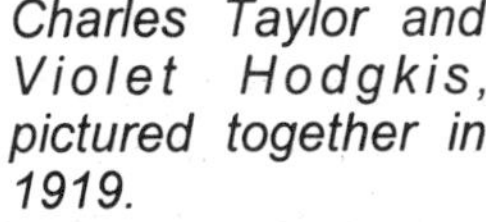

Charles Taylor and Violet Hodgkis, pictured together in 1919.

Despite the initial setback of losing Charles so young, the Taylors went on to have six more children, following very much in the footsteps of Charles' own parents. Alice was born in 1924, the year before her elder brother's death. Then came Albert, Alec, Irene, Thomas and William.

The year following the death of the young Charles, was the year of the General Strike, which struck a severe blow to many communities - the miners among them. There was much hardship and families were forced to dig out coal for their own bunkers to provide fuel for cooking and heating. It was not a practice which went down well with the mine owners and there were harsh sentences for those unfortunate enough to be caught. The Taylors were no exception. They, too, had to dig out their own coal, but were lucky enough not to get caught.

When the General Strike came to an end, the miners found themselves working a two or three-day week. For Charles, with a growing family to support, this was not enough to make ends meet, and he also found employment at the Woodman Inn. His work involved all the odd jobs, like changing barrels, collecting up the glasses, throwing out the drunks at closing time and many other tasks. Despite the hard lives they led bringing up their young family, the Taylors generally had a happy family, typical of the hundreds living in the area at the time.

Thomas, the second youngest child, was born on 29th January, 1932, and was a mischievous lad. Named after his grandfather, to his family he was known simply as Tom, but his friends soon adopted the local slang name for Thomas - 'Tucker'. This derived undoubtedly after the 'Little Tommy Tucker' who sang for his supper in the nursery rhyme. He always had a cheeky smiling face and made friends easily. Like his brothers and sisters, he got on well with all the other children in the area.

His younger brother, Bill, remembers those days well.... *"As a child my first recollection is sitting on the steps of our Quarry Street home and looking at the glow in the distance as they bombed Sheffield. As kids we would all go round with one another, tying front doors together, playing marbles, climbing, playing kick can, hide-and-seek and even stuffing newspapers up drainpipes and setting light to them.*

We weren't well off. Dad was the family cobbler, fixing all the shoes, and my mother took in washing to help make ends meet. Mother was the driving force behind the family. We never saw a lot of our dad when we were young because he was always out working. This probably explains why we had more compassion for my mother than for my father. We weren't budding Einsteins in our family, but we were intelligent enough to know what life was all about and to make the most of what you've got. I think everybody did that."

When Tommy was only a few months old he had a close brush with death. He was playing on a rug in front of the fire when he mistook a piece of coke for a sweet and popped it into his mouth. He swallowed it and began choking and turning blue. His mother panicked and ran into the street screaming *"He's gone! He's gone"*! Luckily, his dad came running in, swiftly turned him upside down and smacked him on the back. Thomas eventually coughed up the piece of coke, much to the relief of the family. This could possibly explain why his mother tended to have a particularly soft spot for him. Even years later when he was in the Army, she used to send him cakes and gifts.

Because his father was working at the Woodman the only time they got together as a family was on a Sunday. In the summer they would go down to the canal for a picnic and a swim, along with the other families in the street. Every Whitsun holiday everybody would put on their Sunday best and visit all the aunts and uncles, to show off their best clothes.

Tommy's first school was Burton Road Junior and Infant School. As a pupil he was nothing outstanding academically, but like the rest of the Taylors, he was no fool either. Throughout his time at Burton Road he remained in the 'B' classes. At the age of 11 he sat his School Certificate to decide which school he should move to next. Particularly bright pupils who passed their School Certificate were sent to the local grammar school. Needless to say, Tommy ended up going the Raley Secondary Modern.

For whatever faults Raley may have had, the one jewel in its crown was that it boasted excellent sports facilities and, in that respect, was the envy of many other schools in the area. There were rugby and football pitches, a well equipped gymnasium plus an indoor swimming pool. The latter, in particular, was something of a rarity at the time. Champion shot-putter Arthur Rowe and cricket umpire Dickie Bird were both former Raley pupils.

The family, by this time, had moved yet again, from No.4 Quarry Street to No.4 St.Helens Avenue. The family lived in this house for many years. It's still there today and has barely changed since the Taylors first moved in. The year was 1941.

By now, Tommy was starting to take a keen interest in football, but his only involvement with the game, up to the War period, had been playing on the streets as a small boy. But at Raley, there were grass pitches and excellent tuition from the sports teacher, as well as a great deal of natural talent. It was not long before Tommy was picked to play for the school team.

After a series of good, solid displays for the school side, he was chosen to play for Barnsley Boys, appearing for this side for two seasons - 1944-5 and 1945-6. He spent his first season as centre forward while in the second, he played at left back. Nobody seems to know why he played in this unfamiliar position for a whole season. Tommy, himself, was not keen in this position, but he was proud to be representing his local boys side.

He gained his first ever mention in a local newspaper while playing in his first season for Barnsley Boys. It was following a match in December, 1944 when they played South Elmsall Boys. The article stated that: *"The game was played on a very muddy pitch in very poor conditions. It was Taylor, Barnsley's centre forward, who finally put them ahead, scoring with a good shot with the goalkeeper unsighted."*

These were the first competitive games in which he ever played and he enjoyed them immensely. His mum and dad never failed to go and cheer him on and they weren't slow either in shouting abuse at anyone they thought was giving Tommy a hard time - including the referee! From this first acknowledgement he rarely failed to get a mention in the local papers. The games were played on the local grammar school pitches, and even occasionally at Frickley Colliery F.C. New Years Day, 1945 was a very special day for Tommy. For, on that day, he played his first ever game at the Barnsley ground, Oakwell, in a match against Leicester Boys. He had a great start to his career, scoring the first goal in a game which ended in a 2-2 draw.

Edward Parkinson, Headmaster at Raley, recalls: *"I remember Tommy when he was 13 years old playing for the Barnsley School team in the period just after the war. There was no competitive schoolboy football in those days, but Tommy was typical of those teachers and boys alike who played inter-town friendlies for the sheer love of it. Tommy was not very tall and for his 13 years he was the smallest boy in the team, but there was never any doubt on account of his lack of inches about his selection. For he was always brimming with energy and enthusiasm. Cheerful, happy and contented, he was the ideal type for a representative for the town."*

BARNSLEY & DISTRICT SCHOOLS FOOTBALL ASSOCIATION.

AT OAKWELL

(By kind permission of the Directors).

BARNSLEY & DISTRICT BOYS v. LEICESTER BOYS

NEW YEAR'S DAY, JANUARY 1st, 1945.

BARNSLEY & DISTRICT BOYS (White, Red Collar & Cuffs)

R .   1 BIRDSALL   L

(Grammar School)

2 LEDGER   3 JOHNSON

(Raley School)   (Grammar School)

4 COOKSON   5 GREEN   6 WALLACE

(Grammar School)   (Longcar Central)   (Junior Tech. School)

8 NEWTON   10 DONNACHIE (Capt.)

(Grammar School)   (Junior Tech. School)

7 WILSON for WILLIAMS   9 TAYLOR   11 SENIOR

(Grammar School)   (Raley School)   (Darton Modern)

Referee :   Linesmen :

Mr. G. SUNDERLAND   Mr. D. GOODYEAR.

Mr. D. LAMBERT.

12 BRENNAN   14 GULLIVER   16 PRESTON

13 HALLAM   15 BAXTER

17 LANCASTER   18 LENNARD   19 BROOKS

20 GARRATT   21 REECE

L   22 SMITH   R

LEICESTER BOYS (Maroon).   KICK-OFF 2-30.

P R O G R A M M E — Price 1d.

Probably the first programme in which the name of Tommy Taylor featured.
He scored one of the goals in this representative match.

By now nothing else but football mattered as far as Tommy was concerned. Although he never had any intentions of becoming a full-time professional, and at the time he was playing for the school he did not even possess a pair of boots! He had to borrow them from anybody who was willing to lend him some.

Not long before he left school, Tommy was due to play for the school team, but he had forgotten to acquire boots. The teacher at the time told him if he wanted to play he would have to play in clogs. Tommy refused, so the teacher sent him home. On future occasions, when he had all his kit with him and wanted to play - he never got a game! Even when his younger brother, Bill (who was also a good player) was ready to be selected for the school side, he was unsuccessful, simply because he was Tommy's brother - another Taylor! Tommy never forgot this. Years later, when he had made the grade, Tommy walked past his former teacher one day in town and totally ignored him. An attitude that was totally out of character.

Tommy left school as a 14-year-old in 1946, just as the war had come to an end, but not for him a fairy tale beginning to a professional career as a footballer. Like hundreds of other school-leavers in that part of the world at that time he went straight to the pit. Although he never actually worked down the mine, for he worked above ground on the screens, sorting out the mud from the coal. This was at Wharncliff Colliery 1.2.3. There were other jobs around, but they had to be found, and the easy way out was to go and work at the local pithead. In any event when all your friends worked there and it paid well, why bother looking elsewhere? So Tommy settled down to this familiar life-style. He worked at Wharncliff for almost two years and not once did the thought of a career as a professional footballer enter his head. The only time he played football were the local kick-arounds with his pals.

By this time, Tommy had started knocking around with a group of lads who were to become his best friends. Bob Nicholls, Joe Harvey, Keith Hibberd, Jimmy Cooper, Bob McCormick and Harry England were all close to Tommy, but none more so than Harry England. A lovely man now approaching his 60th birthday, he gets around with the aid of a walking stick and four steel hip joints, the result of more than 30 years' hard graft as a borer at North Gawber Colliery.

Like the Taylors', the Englands' had a good background in football. Harry's brother Alf was a talented wing half who, when he left school, went to play under the legendary Major Frank Buckley at Wolves. There followed spells playing for Barnsley, Mansfield and Worksop Town, before starting his 15 year association with Brian Clough and Peter Taylor as a top scout with Brighton and Nottingham Forest. Another player in the family was Harry's uncle, Frank Gallacher, who played for Barnsley in the 30's before moving on to join Bristol Rovers. Harry and Tommy first met at Burton Road, where they began swapping football cards. Eventually, they were to be inseparable. Harry's mother, Margaret, became like a second mother to Tommy. Of all the boys who visited the England household, Tommy was without doubt her favourite.

Harry probably knew Tommy better than anyone else, and he has many fond memories: *"Tommy virtually lived at my mother's house, especially during the six-week summer holiday. Even when he was playing for United and England, he would always come round. There was a gang of us going around then and we always drank and played football together. We could never let Tommy and Bob McCormick be on the same side, because they were too good. My mum bought us what she thought was a football, but it was a rugby ball. We blew it up and Tommy could still dribble past us all. He always had lots of tricks up his sleeve. Two of his favourites were where he would stand in front of a bucket, jump up and balance on the rims. Not only that but he could do it backwards as well.*

Once we were walking down the street and he had this trick where he would kick the back of his heel, making himself look drunk. Someone saw him and reported him to Angus Seed, the Barnsley manager. So he had to go and explain himself.

The bog was the place where we all played football. They've built houses on it now. On Saturday we would go into town and buy a couple of records and then go for a game of snooker. After that we would go to the Civic Hall and pay a shilling for our dinner. Afterwards there would be some more snooker, but it was a kid's paradise around here then, though. We had two woods, the River Don and the Dearne, and we would go swimming in the canal in the summer.

Tommy was never the aggressive type, but he could take care of himself. I once read somewhere that he left Barnsley just in time because he was getting in with the drinking crowd. That's rubbish! Believe me, Tommy could drink. We were brought up on it round here, but he always put football first. He would put on a stone in weight in the close season, but he would always go back to Old Trafford two weeks before anybody else, running around the pitch trying to work the extra weight off. When he became famous, he tended to get pestered. Once his dad brought two referees to see him and when I shouted upstairs to him to get up, he refused and went back to sleep. He didn't want to know.

My uncle, Frank and Auntie Beatie, ran a pub in Bradford called the Horse and Jockey and we would go up there for weeks at a time. Actually, that was the place he went to when he came home from South America, I think he just wanted to get away from it all sometimes. In fact, my brother Alf, bought us our first pair of proper boots. I'll never forget them. They were called Mansfield Hotspurs. We would sit for ages with our feet in buckets of cold water so they'd be a good fit. He was always a generous type and he always made sure he got his family and friends tickets for any games. Bob Nicholls had an old Austin hearse and we used to go to Manchester on a Saturday to watch him play and sometimes he'd come back home with us.

He told me once he would go to Italy if I'd have gone with him, but it never happened, of course. He was a happy-go-lucky person who always had a smile on his face. In fact, I only saw him cry once. It was in the back of a taxi and the tears were streaming down his face. I said 'What's up?' and he said 'Nothing'. I never did find out why. I'll tell you something, every time football is talked about around here, his name is mentioned. Whether it's the young kids or the older folk. He'll never be forgotten in Smithies."

Football was not Tommy's only preoccupation when he wasn't on the football field or in the snooker hall. Another favourite pastime in his younger days was riding horses. Harry Kay was a local entrepreneur who you could guarantee would be around if there was any money to be made. Peter, his son, was a professional show-jumper and, in the 60's and 70's his other son became the famous wrestler Tally Ho Kay. Tommy, Bill and Harry used to go and muck out the stables, make up jumps and ride the horses - something which Tommy loved. It did not rest there, for so hooked were Tommy and his mates that they used to go to various shows up and down the country selling ice-cream with Harry Kay. In their younger days, Tommy's brothers - Albert and Alec - worked for Mr.Kay doing any odd jobs that needed doing.

Bill remembers: *"Another routine of ours back then was on a Saturday morning. We'd play football, go home for a quick wash and then charge off to the Regent for a quick game of snooker. After that it was on to the pictures - something everybody used to do then. On the way home there were three fish and chip shops and we'd call in at every one. Sunday mornings everybody would be out for a game of football on the narrow pitch at the end of Richard Road."*

It was really through a piece of bad luck rather than good fortune that eventually led to Tommy turning to football for a career and becoming a pro. During a kick-around on the bog with Harry England one Saturday morning, Tommy's uncle Tucker came up to ask him if he would be interested in playing for Smithies United because they were desperate for players for a game against Cudworth North End in the Beckett Hospital Cup.

Smithies was a local pub side based at the Woodman Inn, the pub run by Tommy's aunt Esther Raynor, who was herself a keen football fan. The team played in the local Nelson League. One of the players, local fireman Harry Brown, was in the pub a couple of nights earlier worrying about getting a team together for the game. So Harry's failure to find enough players gave Tommy his chance for a career in football. He played well enough in the first leg, scoring one goal, and in the second leg helped the team to a 2-2 draw. He only played three games for the side.

At these games was an ex-footballer, Horace Plant, who as well as running a local youth team did some part-time scouting for Barnsley Football Club. Tommy was asked if he would be interested in going along to Oakwell a couple of weeks later for a trial. He was also approached by a scout from Hull City, but he turned down the request as it would simply be too far for him to travel. Tommy was also recommended to Barnsley by another local scout, Harry Wass (the club had eleven scouts in the area at that time). He did well enough at the Barnsley trial to be offered a job on the groundstaff. For a 16-year-old destined to become one of the best centre-forwards in the country, Smithies United were paid the princely sum of £10. For the young Tommy Taylor that £10 transfer fee was to change his life for ever. Life would never ever be the same again, for that sum of money and that offer, were to take him from one world into something completely different. Tommy had quite unknowingly at that stage taken the first step in a career that was to make him a household name the length and breadth of the country.

February 1948. Tommy., with family and friends, celebrate his signing for Barnsley.
He was sixteen years old.

CHAPTER 2

WELCOME TO OAKWELL

Barnsley football club, originally Barnsley St.Peters, was founded in 1887 (the Jubilee Year of Queen Victoria) by the Rev.Tiverton Preedy (a curate of St. Peters' Church) who later laboured for many years in Pentonville, at the All Saints Mission.

From very humble beginnings, the club soon made headway, gaining admission to the Second Division eleven years later, and later startled the Football World in 1910 by reaching the final of the F.A. Cup. They finally won the coveted trophy following a replay at Bramall Lane in 1912, by beating West Bromwich Albion one nil in extra time.

During the first year the club rented the Oakwell ground from a Mr. Arthur Senior and played friendly matches on it. In the 1890/91 season the local Football Association was formed and St. Peters' joined the local competition. Still known as St. Peters', the club entered the F.A. Cup in 1893 for the first time. St. Peters joined the Midland League for the 1895/96 season, and in their second campaign they changed the club name to 'Barnsley F.C.' On their election to the Second Division of the Football League (in 1898), they turned professional and changed their colours from Blue and White stripes to Red shirts and White shorts. The club purchased the Oakwell Ground for £1,376 in 1907.

The Club has always been known mainly as a Second Division side but down the years it boasted a string of star players, including many Internationals. Throughout its history though, it has had to sit back and sell them, in order to stay afloat financially. The Club came very close to Division One in 1921 but missed out on promotion despite scoring more goals than anyone else. At that time the team could boast Frank Barson, an outstanding centre-half who, like Tommy, was a superb header of the ball and after leaving Oakwell he played for Manchester United and England. Ernest Hine, a prolific goalscorer with a tremendous shot was also capped four times for his country, and like Barson later played at Old Trafford. Fred Tilson and Eric Brook, before signing for Manchester City, were two stylish Barnsley forwards who also went on to become Internationals.

During the Second World War, Barnsley played in a regional league, and despite having the War Cup to play for, these years were unfruitful, but it did throw up one tremendous prospect - George Robledo. In his first peacetime match, at twenty years of age, when the League resumed after the war, he scored all three goals in his side's 3-2 win over Nottingham Forest. Another player of the day was Jimmy Baxter, who later went on to play alongside Tom Finney at Preston and was in the side that lost to West Bromwich Albion in the 1954 F.A. Cup Final. Johnny Kelly, a tricky, often brilliant Winger, was also a Scottish International. In the 1948-49 season, manager Angus Seed, with a reputation for spotting young talent, went over to Ireland to recruit an unknown youngster by the name of Danny Blanchflower. The Wing Half had been playing for Glentoran and Barnsley had to fight off a lot of competition from other English clubs to secure his signature for a £6,500 fee. Blanchflower soon matured into a class player and whilst at Barnsley he was capped for Ireland alongside his club colleague, goalkeeper Pat Kelly.

Looking back it seems hard to imagine that with such a wealth of talent at the club it never did well in Cup competitions and always seemed to be such an average Second Division side. Despite the lack of real success the club can boast of having many outstanding players on its books, including many Internationals.

On February 7th 1948, a young, raw, sixteeen year old prospect named Tommy Taylor walked into the Oakwell ground, two weeks after guesting for Smithies United in the Beckett Hospital Cup. Tommy had been nearly two years away from the game, for he had been working at the mine. For many players these years were meant to be crucial to a youngsters development, if he hoped to become a professional footballer. Luckily the young Taylor had enough natural talent to come through his trial and he was offered a job on the groundstaff.

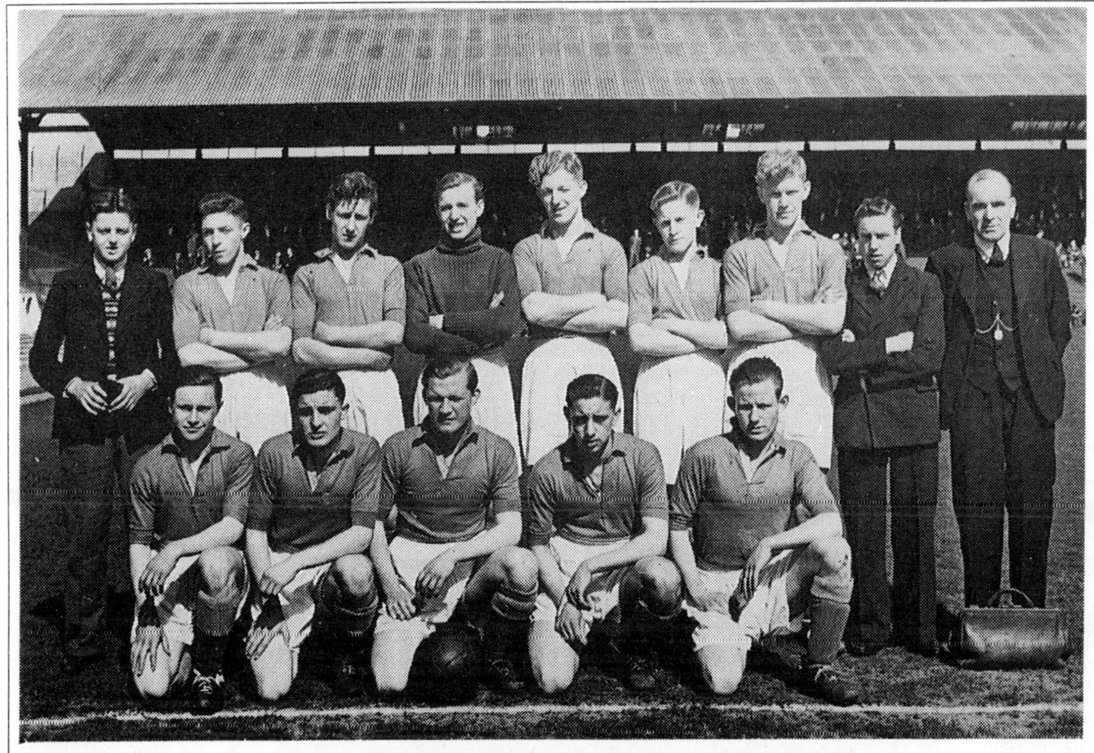

The Barnsley 'A' team and groundstaff,
soon after Tommy (back row, left) signed for the club.

The key person in the development of young players at Oakwell at this time was Johnny Steele. He was then Youth Team Trainer, before becoming Manager, Secretary, General Manager, Director, Vice President, and in the years before the War he had been a brilliant ball-playing Inside Forward for the club. Nobody can have played so many roles at one club, and it is no wonder they call him 'Mr.Barnsley'. In his days as Manager he once tried to sign a talented youngster from St. Johnstone called Alex Ferguson - the current Manchester United Manager.

He looks back affectionately to the days when a small rather skinny lad from Smithies came to the club. *"We had a tremendous thing at Barnsley at the time. At one time we had five teams, the first team and reserves, one in the Yorkshire League, one in the Hatchard and one in the Northern Intermediate. There were perhaps 40 or 50 players who would train. The amateurs came and trained on Mondays and Wednesdays, part-time pros on Tuesdays and Thursdays. On Friday everybody would come in and stud the boots, you know, there was always some activity day and night. Our training always ended up with a game and it was in these games that we really got to know what was what, as regard any talent. But when it comes to Tommy, it was obvious he was going to be a good player. He was a fantastic character and as a lad he was very mischievous.*

He'd throw senior players' socks in the baths and throw bangers around on firework nights. He was very high spirited and at the end of the day he would often hang around the dressing rooms not wanting to go home, he really got to love the place. At times he could be boisterous, as opposed to some of the other players who were a bit shy, and we really got to love him here.

As a player he didn't have everything, he was long striding and a great header of the ball, but he never had what we call 'quick feet', say like John Charles, although he was sure-footed and believe me Tommy could hit a ball. Some say he was a bit clumsy on the ball, but he made up for that with his other great assets.

Angus Seed at the time had great vision and he was mostly responsible for starting the Northern Intermediate League. The idea was to develop and groom young stars and try to put an end to the big transfer dealings which were happening at the time. He always boasted Tommy was its first product. Jimmy Murphy and myself were actually good friends, I'll never forget the time we played United in a Central League Match. At half time we were 2-0 in front and we could all hear him in the dressing room... 'that team of effin colliers are effin beating you' - he would swear like a trooper - and in the second half they played us off the park, but we just held on.

Tommy was a very eager learner, in fact the only thing I can ever remember really coaching him on was his turning, the rest just came naturally."

Barnsley F.C. 1952/53. (Back row): Jarman, Smith, Betts, Hough, Seed (Manager), May, Dougle, Shotton (Trainer). (Front row): Kay, Chapple, Taylor, McMorran, Kelly, McNeil.

So Tommy really enjoyed his early days at Oakwell. It must have been something of a dream for him, for he surely must have thought he was set for nothing more than a career at the pit. The only time he played, after leaving school, were the kick-arounds with his pals on the bog. He never even made any attempt to play for the colliery team during his time there.

His first year was spent in the Hatchard League with the 'B' Team. The League was mainly made up of Sheffield Steelworks teams and was open to all age groups, and although it could be quite rough at times the football was of a high standard. The Northern Intermediate was only open to 18 year-olds or under, and Tommy only actually played in this League four or five times. As a groundstaff boy he did all the usual jobs, repairing the pitch, painting the stands, and cleaning senior players' boots.

Tommy made friends very easily, during his time at Oakwell, his closest was probably Doug Kelly who, although a year younger, was soon to be pushing for a place in the first team at centre-forward. He talks fondly of his days with a person who not only was a good friend but also his main rival for the number nine jersey. *"Tommy and I became good friends, and we were both an outgoing pair of lads who enjoyed a day at the races or the dogs or even just a pint. After a game we would all go home and get changed and meet back at the ground. There was Tommy, me, Norman Smith, and the two Maurices - Jackson and Hudson.*

1950.
A contented Tommy, perhaps contemplating his future career in football.

I suppose the reason we all hung around together was, despite being the youngest, we were the only ones who weren't married. There were six or seven cinemas in Barnsley and we had passes for all of them. Dillington dog track was another popular haunt, although we didn't like to go out boozing too much because there were always people about who would report you if you had too much ale!

Let me say this. Even if the fellow next to you is a great friend - you went out together and roomed together on away matches like Tommy and me did - you were also rivals, playing for the same position. Life wasn't always a bed of roses as you may think, for as kids on the groundstaff we would have to wash and clean Angus Seeds' car every Monday morning. He had a Spaniel dog and we spent ages trying to get the dog hairs off the seat!

If you asked me what it is I remember most about Tommy, it would be the way he dressed. He was the first person I saw wearing a black shirt. He got his clothes from a shop on the Sheffield Road called 'Collins'. He got them for nothing because in the shop window was a picture of Tommy wearing the clothes as an up-and-coming Barnsley star. He was a very trendy dresser, almost gaudy, he was even wearing crepe soled shoes a year or two before the rock and roll era. He came from a big family and it must have been quite difficult for him to go to Manchester. He always stayed at my house when we were playing away. Sometimes he got bigheaded, but in a nice sort of way, but as a friend he was superb. He was always jaunty, walking with a bounce, with a very laid back attitude to life where nothing seemed to get on top of him. I bet many of today's footballers wish they could be like that."

So Tommy's first games for Barnsley were spent in the B-team in the Hatchard League. Within the year he had worked his way up to the 'A' team, which played in the Yorkshire League. By now it was the 1949-50 season, and it turned out to be very eventful. On July 25th 1949, Tommy signed professional forms, and in the following May he was called up to do his National Service. At that time he had the opportunity not to go into the Army if he so wished, for if you were serving an apprenticeship you were exempt until you were twenty-one. Barnsley Chairman, Joe Richards was also on the local Coal Board Committee and he had set up an arrangement (some said by using cash incentives), whereby young up-and-coming footballers could obtain work at the pit while still enabling them to play football. Tommy declined this offer, for having already nearly two years experience of working at the pit, he didn't want to go back. He also thought the Army would enable him to improve his overall fitness, and he would also get the chance to play in the Forces if he wanted to.

His service commenced on the 25th May, 1950 and he was stationed at Oswestry, where he became *Gunner Taylor 22366853*, of the Royal Artillery. He was later posted to Tonfirnan, Meronethshire in North Wales. It wasn't long before he became an automatic choice for his unit side. He went on to play many times for his Regimental team in Division One of the Welsh League, and also for the Northern Command. In fact his side were League Champions on two consecutive occasions - 1950-51 and 1951-52 -and Tommy had played an important role in the first of these successes.

If he entered the Army a boy he certainly left a man. When he went in he was still rather skinny and a bit on the small side, but the Army did him the world of good, for he soon put on two stone in weight and shot up a couple of inches. During his time, he won medals for sprinting and the long jump. Whilst in the services he played football alongside, and also against, many other fellow Professionals such as Geoff Twentyman, Tommy Hoyland, Jimmy Hill and John Charles.

The Army had two principal Cups at the time, which sides competed for - the Inter-Command Challenge Cup and the Triangular Tournament for the Kentish Cup. This latter competition was held between the British, Belgian and French Armies. The away game in France was Tommy's first trip abroad, and it was here that he realised just what the game of football could offer. His travels also took him for a short trip to Austria, where Tommy was the star of the three match tour. In one game, the Army played a side which contained seven of the Austrian International team, and he scored a 20 minute hat-trick. The team produced an overall 11-3 goal record and the young Taylor took most of the credit.

(Left) A happy Gunner Taylor, and (below), a group picture under canvass. Tommy (third from left) in good company, including Freddie Goodwin (sixth from left) and Dennis Viollet (sitting second from right), who were at Old Trafford at the time, and were to become future team-mates of Tommy.

The schedules were often very hectic with the different XI's not only playing other Army sides but also various League clubs up and down the country. For instance in October 1950, he played for the Army against Aston Villa and Everton, plus games for the Western Command against Sheffield United and the Scottish Command. One of his most memorable games was against the Irish Football League, although he was on the losing side by four goals to two, Tommy was the outstanding player. Most of the big Army games were reported by the National Newspapers and for this game one report read:

> *"The Irish League were cleverer, but the Army played grand go-ahead stuff and led by imbuing Taylor, deputy Centre Forward at Barnsley, gave Matthews and company a stiff grilling. Considering all the representative games played in Belfast this season this was by far the best. Taylors' play alone was worth the admission and the Army's second goal, which he obtained, was worth double. He flicked in a brilliant header from thirty yards, which rebounded off the far post and he was in like a streak to get on top of the loose ball to score."*

It was in fact heading the ball for which Tommy was to become famous. When he was younger he would spend hours practising with his uncle Tucker and the former Barnsley and Manchester United player, Beaumont Asquith, was also undoubtedly an early influence for he too was renowned for his perfect heading ability. The players used to train under the Old Trafford stands, and Tommy would practice his heading with a ball suspended on a rope; the ball being raised higher as the season progressed.

A few weeks before he entered the Army, on 2nd May 1950, Tommy made his first ever appearance in Barnsley's first team. The team had travelled to Scotland to play St. Mirren in the Paisley Charity Cup. 8,000 spectators had turned up at Love Street to see the visitors take the Trophy after Barnsley centre-forward Alec Wright scored the only goal in the 25th minute. Tommy played at inside-right for this game. Johnny Steele insists that Tommy got picked since he was by then a lot stronger physically, but this is probably only partly true. The main reason was doubtless due to Barnsley at the time having a spate of injuries, and some players who were away on International duty. Tommy made his League debut on 7th October 1950, against Grimsby Town. Barnsley's inside-right Griffiths was not fit and Tommy was on leave from the Army at the time. He was just 18. A crowd of just over 18,000 saw Barnsley win 3-1. Tommy had a good game and came close to scoring on two occasions, but the credit went to Cecil McCormack who scored all three goals. That win pushed the team into third position in Division Two, McCormack having then scored 18 goals in 12 games. Tommy wasn't picked the following week but in the next home game he had another chance to prove himself and he took it. Queens Park Rangers were the visitors and with Jimmy Baxter injured, Tommy for once overshadowing McCormack, scored a superb hat-trick in the side's convincing 7-0 win. At the time, the Army had priority over players when it came to matches and this limited Tommy to 12 first team outings that season, during which he scored 7 goals.

On the occasions that he was picked for the first team, he had to be picked up from his Army Camp in North Wales. This job was usually done by Johnny Steele and club Masseur Fred Semley. Together they would travel, regardless of the weather, to collect him despite the journey taking nearly four hours. Tommy had to make his own arrangements to get back to his camp, and he usually went by train. Meanwhile, Barnsley could only manage a final place of 15th in the League that season. The 1951-52 campaign was going to prove a very disappointing one, not only for Tommy, but also for Barnsley Football Club. Danny Blanchflower had been sold to Aston Villa and Cecil McCormack, who the previous season had scored 33 goals (a record which still stands today), was also sold. Tommy meanwhile - who was still in the Army - suffered an injury which many people thought would end his football career.

Amongst the honours at the end of the 1950/51 season (Tommy - 2nd from right, back row)

Tommy (front row, 2nd left), with the great John Charles, (2nd from right, back row), Tommy netted a hat-trick in the 5-1 Army victory over the Carinthians (Austria).

A relaxed team gathering for the Cup-tie at Northampton (January 1951)
There were no smiles from Tommy (back, centre) after the surprise 3-1 defeat.

He was playing in a match for the 55th Training Regiment at Litchfield, against a side which was selected from the North Staffordshire Regiment. Tommy later said that this was the roughest game he ever played. During the game the ball came across the penalty area and he jumped for it along with the goalkeeper, but as he fell the opposing goalkeeper landed on top of him, falling awkwardly on Tommy's knee. Severe cartilage trouble was diagnosed as well as torn ligaments and a cracked bone. He was taken back home to Barnsley, admitted to the Becketts Hospital where he underwent two operations, and his leg was put in plaster for many months. He was out of action for eleven months and by the time he got over the injury his Army days were virtually over.

Back at Oakwell, there was certainly a feeling that he would never play again . Fred Semley, the club masseur, thought Tommy should forget about any hopes he might have about making a return to League football. Finally, as a last resort, Tommy travelled to Newcastle to see a specialist, who much to the relief of the Taylor family was able to offer his assurance that he would be able to sort the injury out.

Tommy, at times, felt he would never play again and he felt like giving up any dreams he may have had of making a return to professional football. His mother, however, gave him a great deal of encouragement and together they worked out a routine which would hopefully get him at least on his feet. For 30 minutes, at four-hourly intervals, he would put weights on his leg, lay in front of the fire, and lift his leg. He carried out these exercises day in day out until he could walk around unaided.

The Army and his injury had limited Tommy to only 4 League appearances and no goals in the 1951/52 season. He was eventually discharged on 15th June 1952. His discharge papers read:

"Mr. Taylor is a clean, smart man, with a quiet but cheerful disposition. He did any job given him to the best of his ability."

With his injury clearing up and no National Service Tommy now had a few months to get fit for the very eventful 1952-53 season.

Although during the two previous seasons Tommy played mainly at inside-left, this campaign saw him in his favourite position at centre- forward. However, any hopes the club may have had for some success had all but disappeared by Christmas. The season ended up being one of the worst in the club's history, not least the first half of the campaign when the team could only manage five wins.

Doug Kelly recalls: *"We had a bad start to that particular season, and after about 3 weeks Angus Seed brought in five or six players from the youth team, including myself. We lost to Everton 3-2; Tommy scored one and me the other. We played Sheffield United the following Saturday and lost 3-1. For the following game against Rotherham, Tommy was dropped by Mr. Seed, probably for the only time in his career, and he was put into the reserve side who were playing Manchester United on the Wednesday. The centre-half that day for United was Mark Jones. I knew Mark very well because I played with him in the school team and also for Don-on-Dearne Boys. Anyhow, Marks' strength was always in the air, but that particular day Tommy played him off the park and Mark never saw the ball. Tommy went on to score a hat-trick. I can remember it as if it was yesterday, and I believe Jimmy Murphy saw something in Tommy which no one else could see. Anyhow, for the following League games, Angus Seed rubbed my name off the team sheet and put Tommy's on, for he had played himself back into the side."*

It proved to be a season of highs and lows. Jimmy Baxter had moved to Preston North End and the team failed to win their remaining 23 matches. The season wasn't all doom and gloom though, for on January 10th, there was a game to savour in the F.A. Cup 3rd round tie against Brighton. After half an hour Brighton were leading 3-0 with goals from Owens, Howard and Reed and a crowd of over 17,000 was stunned into silence. With the League season going badly wrong it now seemed that the Reds were going to be unceremoniously dumped out of the F.A. Cup competition in embarrassing fashion on their own ground. It is said that some Barnsley fans even went home at half-time with the team 3-0 down, and apparently out.

A shrewd position switch by Skipper Norman Smith helped to bring about a remarkable transformation. Smith himself moved to full-back to try and contain Brighton's outside-left, Howard, who had been giving Barnsley's Tom Blenkinsop a torrid time. Arthur Kaye went to inside-forward and Tommy Lumley went to right-half.

In the 62nd minute Kaye pulled one back with a curling shot, two minutes later Tommy scored the second, and with fifteen minutes remaining, Oakwell became a cauldron of noise when Eddie McMorran scored the equaliser. The fans sensed that a remarkable victory was in the air, and sure enough with barely three minutes to go a poor clearance from the goalkeeper was headed down by McMorran for Tommy to hit home the dramatic winner and his second goal. This game provided the best Cup fightback in Barnsley's long Cup-fighting history. The season ended with the team eventually being relegated to Division Three North.

The club had picked up only five points out of the last 46 available, scoring 47 goals and conceding a record 108. Tommy, though, was playing very well for he netted 19 goals in 28 appearances. It was clear to see that he had 'arrived', and he was beginning to catch the eye of many League clubs in the country. Before the end of the season, both Eddie McMorran and Tommy would be playing elsewhere.

There had been talk of a transfer for several months, prior to Tommy's departure in March 1953. The Club at this time, although financially in difficulty, had stated that it was only interested in fighting the relegation battle at the foot of Division Two and not in selling Tommy, although at first they said if they were relegated they would part with him.

There were many clubs in the chase for his signature, the principal three initially were Manchester United, Derby County and Middlesbrough. The latter's manager, Walter Rowley, had tried to sign Tommy several weeks earlier to cure his centre-forward problem, but was turned down. On Wednesday 25th February 1953, then Chairman Joe Richards, issued the following statement *"If we go down into the Third Division we shall keep Taylor and if we go out of the League altogether we shall keep him."*

Despite all the speculation Tommy was having a good season. On October 4th 1952 he scored twice in a 5-1 demolition of Hull City, Then came two more including a penalty in a 3-2 victory over Bury. Tommy was 21 on 29th January 1953.

Tommy (bottom left), with (left to tight) Maurice Hudson, Norman Smith, Maurice Jackson and Doug Kelly (bottom right) en-route to Plymouth, where Barnsley lost 1-0.

The team travelled to Plymouth for an F.A. cup-tie, and despite losing he celebrated his birthday with his team mates at the local nightspot *'The Seven of Clubs'*. On the way back to Barnsley, on the train, Angus Seed was taken ill, and he was eventually taken off at Gloucester and put straight into hospital. Seed died on 7th February, the day after his 60th birthday, and also the day that Tommy missed a penalty in the last few moments of the game against Rotherham, that would not only have given him his hat-trick but also earned his team a 3-3 draw. Tommy only played three more games for Barnsley, during which he scored two more goals. His last ever game for the club was on the 14th February 1953, in a 1-1 draw against Lincoln City, which was played in five inches of snow.

Tommy attacking in a way that was to become his hallmark - with his head.
Action from a Yorkshire derby match, Barnsley versus Huddersfield Town at Oakwell.

By the end of February rumours were rife that Tommy would soon be on his way. At one stage 17 clubs, 14 in the First Division and three in the Second were interested. This renewed interest was following a decision by the Barnsley Directors to eventually put him on the list. The Directors, headed by Joe Richards met one evening in a local hotel, but it was a meeting they had been trying to avoid for several weeks. After three hours, Joe Richards came out of the hotel where he was met by local pressmen. He said *"At long last we have decided to place Taylor on the transfer list. It was a hard decision to make. We shall now negotiate with those clubs which have made enquiries."*

Sunderland, West Ham, Wolves and Sheffield Wednesday were among some of the other clubs interested. Sheffield Wednesday had wanted to sign Tommy as a replacement for the legendary goalscorer Derek Dooley, who sadly had to have his leg amputated following gangrene being diagnosed after an injury.

Of all the clubs it was to be Manchester United and Cardiff City who looked most likely to get his signature. The first fee mentioned was £20,000 and it looked like it wouldn't be long before the record fee of £34,000, paid by Sheffield Wednesday to Notts County for the services of Jackie Sewell, would be broken.

It ended up being a game of cat and mouse between Busby and Cardiff's Cyril Speirs. Herbert Merrett, Cardiff's Chairman, confirmed the Welsh side had offered £35,000, a new record. Barnsley accepted but Tommy didn't. The only reason being that, despite the money, Cardiff was simply too removed from home, and if he had to go it was going to be to a club which wasn't too far away. The huge amounts being talked about were enough to frighten off Derby manager, Stuart McMillan, who was staying in Barnsley at the time.

A mad scramble ensued in the bid to sign Tommy Taylor

It's said that Jimmy Murphy watched Tommy on at least seventeen occasions, although this is probably somewhat exaggerated. Johnny Carey was also asked to go and watch Tommy play and he remembers: *"I was very pleased when Matt signed Tommy. He had previously asked me to go to watch the Barnsley v Leicester game at Filbert Street to keep an eye on the young centre forward called Taylor. I reported back to Matt, and told him I was very impressed, and I felt he would be a good goalscorer for Manchester United. Matt turned round to me and said I was the ninth person to recommend him. My prediction was correct of course."* One thing is certain, as soon as Busby himself saw Taylor, he knew he was the man for the job. He told his Directors it was going to be very difficult to sign him, and he warned that they may have to break the transfer record to get him.

Matt and Jimmy had gone to Barnsley and set up headquarters at the Royal Hotel. They stayed there for four days and nights, wondering what Cardiff's Cyril Speirs was up to. One evening Jimmy and Matt went to the cinema, as they went in Jimmy gave the Usherette two half-crowns and said *"If you see a tall man coming in wearing a camel haired coat let me know won't you?"* Sure enough Speirs came in, and Jimmy was notified. The saga came to an end when Joe Richards told Busby *"The fee for Taylor is £30,000, pay me that fee and he's yours."* This was all very well, but at the end of the day it was down to the player, and at first Tommy refused to talk to anyone. It was the biggest manhunt in post war football and Tommy was soon labelled the Golden Boy of 1953.

Meanwhile, Tommy had made a statement in the Barnsley Chronicle, in which he said *"I don't like the idea of leaving a sinking ship, Barnsley have been very good to me, but what couldn't they do with a big sum of money. I don't want to leave Barnsley. I like the place, the club, the players and my girlfriend is here and all my family, but I also know there's the money side to it, I will decide by Tuesday."*

Eventually, following a training session, Tommy told Joe Richards that he would like to be interviewed by representatives of Manchester United. He went to the Royal Hotel and talked terms.

Apparently his only conditions were for tickets for his family and friends, and a special request was made by Tommy to enable him to still live in Barnsley and continue to train at Oakwell. Although Busby agreed, this idea never materialised, and after signing, Tommy moved straight to Manchester.

During the first meeting, Tommy hadn't signed and after leaving Matt and Jimmy he went back to Oakwell to meet up with Doug Kelly and a few others, and they all went off to the Pictures. Half-way through the film a message flashed up on the screen *"Tommy Taylor please go to Oakwell"* and that evening Tommy signed for Manchester United.

He never haggled over terms, despite all the rumours going around at the time that Matt had used all sorts of inducements to persuade Tommy. Talking about the transfer Busby said *"A certain amount of diplomacy and a dash of psychology were needed to get Taylor!!"* During the signing Busby had even knocked a pound off the original fee so Tommy wasn't labelled a £30,000 player. He gave the pound to assistant secretary, Lily Wilby, who was serving tea in the boardroom at the time.

The following day, Eddie Hall, sports writer to the Star Newspaper wrote: *"The Oakwell transfer boom which I forecast two weeks ago has been the most memorable incident of the season in the world of football buying and selling. It will certainly be remembered as the most memorable week in the history of the Oakwell club.*

It was remarkable that a young player, Tommy Taylor, should have been indifferent to a move which would bring the football world at his feet. At the same time Tommy's team-mate Eddie McMorran was also reluctant to leave Barnsley, who are relegation candidates. Directors were in two minds about transferring the two, who could help save the club from the drop, but if they held on too long they would miss the transfer deadline. The departure of Taylor and McMorran has given Barnsley the financial means to live and fight another day."

When Tommy departed for United, Barnsley had no Manager, with the death of Angus Seed, and former England Wing Half, Tim Ward, was soon appointed to the post. Although the team was relegated, they bounced back straight into the Second Division the following season.

Years later, Cecil McCormack still suffered pangs of remorse for telling Tommy a year before his eventual departure that if he left Barnsley then Manchester United should be the club to try to join. One or two members of his family had also urged him to go to United as they had a good reputation with young players. Tommy was only 21 at the time, and they were quite well off financially.

So on 4th March 1953, Tommy became a Manchester United player. He had scored 28 goals in 46 games for his home club, not in any way earth shattering statistics, but as Doug Kelly said, no one at Barnsley would ever have said that Tommy would be good enough for England, but Jimmy and Matt knew otherwise. The cheque for £29,999 was the biggest Oakwell had ever received, the previous record was £24,000 paid by Newcastle for the Robledo Brothers and it was certainly the biggest that United had ever handed over, but the transaction proved to be one of the best they ever made.

February 1953. When Tommy signed for United, Barnsley team-mate Eddie McMorran moved on to Doncaster Rovers.

Tommy arrived in Manchester for the first time on Thursday March 5th 1953. He had received a telegram early that morning saying that a B.B.C. Television Newsreel crew would be there to film him. Is this exclusive footage gathering dust somewhere?

He travelled across from Barnsley along with his then girlfriend, Norma Curtis. The pair were met off the train by Jimmy Murphy and it was he who gave them a tour of Old Trafford and showed them where his digs were situated.

As they went into the dressing rooms, sweeping up was a sixteen year old up and coming winger, Albert Scanlon, who like Doug Kelly at Barnsley remembers the day Tommy made an impression on Jimmy Murphy. *"I saw Tommy before he made his debut at United"*, Albert remembers, *"I was taken as twelfth man to Barnsley, and in those days twelfth man never played. There was me, Jimmy Murphy, Bill Inglis, Bert Whalley.*

We'd only just kicked off about ten minutes when Jimmy appeared in the dug out. All of a sudden he became fascinated by this centre forward. Now in those days you could go and give the 'keeper a good barge, not like today when they're well protected by the refs whistle. So there was Jimmy on his Senior Service and Bill on his Woodbines and all Jimmy could say was 'look at him, look at him'. That's all he was interested in and he must have kept on about Tommy for the full ninety minutes. Anyhow, we got beat and you must understand that when you got beat it was Bill Inglis you had to worry about because he would lose his two quid bonus, he'd throw things about and go for ages without talking to anybody. So after the game, Jimmy was glowing and he went up to big Gordon Clayton, our goalkeeper, who was only a lad then like me, maybe sixteen or seventeen, and he asked what he thought of their Centre Forward. Gordon said 'not bad, a bit rough and ready but not bad'. Jimmy looked up at him and said 'not bad, is that all you can say, not bad, well that's maybe so but he put the fear of effin God into you didn't he?' and he talked about him all the way home.

Anyway, as soon as he came into the dressing room I remember thinking to myself, hello, that's the fella who scored a hat-trick against us not so long ago. Murphy introduced us and he asked what was on tonight. I replied that I was going to Maine Road to watch City play Glasgow Rangers, so he asked me to take Tommy. So we went to the game and afterwards we went to my mum and dad's house in Hulme for some tea, and then I put him on a bus to his digs. He only came to my mothers house the once but he never forgot, he always managed to send her a present every Christmas."

Tommy travelled back to Barnsley that evening quite happy about the way things were working out for him. The following day he caught the train back to Manchester with his suitcase packed, this time to stay for good. It was a big step for him at the time and he was still reluctant to leave his home town but he needn't have worried. He was able to make friends easily and he soon settled in to his new way of life.

When he got off the train he was met by Matt Busby and Johnny Carey as well as the local press. The party were surprised when he stepped off the train with his boots in a tatty brown paper bag.

Friday 6th March 1953. Matt Busby and Johnny Carey meet Tommy off the train at London Road Station, Manchester.

At home with Mum and Dad, the day he signed for Manchester United

At first Tommy lived at Mrs. Watson's, in a large house in Stretford, used by lorry drivers, travelling salesmen as well as up and coming footballers. Other United players who were staying there at the time were Mark Jones, Duncan Edwards, Billy Whelan, Bobby Charlton and Jackie Blanchflower.

On 7th March, 1953 Tommy put on the red shirt of United for the first time for his home debut against Preston. In the game, he managed to put some much needed life into the forward line and he delighted the crowd with his enterprise and ability. He showed a great deal of liveliness from the start and he went on to score two impressive goals. The first one came in the 17th minute from a header. The end result was 5-2 in United's favour, with young David Pegg also scoring a brace in one of his first games for the Club. Tommy linked up very well with Johnny Berry, something they would do for the next four or five years.

TAYLOR ATTACK ALIGHT

GOAL SET

MANCHESTER U. 5   PRESTON N.E. 2

TOMMY TAYLOR, United's £27,000 capture from Barnsley, soon showed his paces against Preston North End and delighted with his enterprise and ability. He put new life into the forward line and scored a brilliant goal in the 17th minute.

Preston were not quite so much in evidence as United, but they drew level in the 29th minute through their centre-forward ... ... United

Matt Busby knew his goalscoring problems had been solved. Stan Pearson and Jack Rowley were, in all honesty, passed their best. Johnny Downie had left Old Trafford in 1953 for Luton Town and Eddie Lewis could never make the centre-forward position his own, and by 1955 he was playing for Preston.

United were dumped out of the F.A. Cup that season by Everton in February so all the team were playing for was a respectable position in the League; they managed 8th. Tommy played ten more games that season, scoring seven goals in eleven appearances. His other goals came against Charlton, both home and away, and against Newcastle. This latter game was significant as it marked the debuts of Dennis Viollet and future United secretary, Les Olive, who was in goal.

More and more youngsters were now being brought into the side and Manchester United now began giving British football fair warning of their rising power. By the end of the season, although occasionally playing at inside-right, Tommy was firmly established in the first team as centre-forward.

Goalscoring Manchester United debutant TOMMY TAYLOR (right) goes up with team-mate ROWLEY and Preston half-back FORBES in a high-flying battle for the ball at Old Trafford.

Back at Mrs Watson's Tommy and Jackie Blanchflower became the best of friends and along with Mark Jones they became the ringleaders who would organise the evenings' activities. They were older than the other lads with more first team experience. Tommy and Jackie would often catch the tram into town to have a good night out, and they were often seen either walking, or staggering, back to their digs. Gordon Clayton recalls, *"We would get back to our digs at around quarter-to-eleven and there would be cornflakes on the table for us, we would eat them and go straight to bed. Some of the lads stayed up half the night playing cards. Most of the nightspots in Manchester were visited. Places like 'The Plaza', where the young Jimmy Saville was assistant manager, 'Cafe Royal', 'Belle Vue', 'Zanzibar', 'The Sportsmens', 'The Cromford Club' - all were popular haunts at one time or another."*

Tommy must have made quite an impression with the England selectors at the close of the 1952-53 season, for as he was walking home one evening he bought a newspaper and reading through it he discovered to his complete surprise, that he had been selected to travel with the England Party for the summer tour of South America. In three short months he had come from a virtual unknown to International level. His rise to the top had indeed been very rapid.

He was part of an 18 man party to play a series of five games, three of which were full Internationals. After travelling to the Argentine Embassy in London to meet up with the rest of the England party, they took a short coach trip to London Airport. The party boarded the B.O.A.C. Argosy, and they settled down for the exhausting 36 hour flight. Tommy had team-mate Johnny Berry for company but it was to be Tom Finney who took Taylor under his wing and the young man became very popular with the other players, he was also the youngest player on the tour.

For Tommy it was unlike anything he had known before. He was given two pounds a day expenses and he enjoyed the luxurious surroundings - swimming pools, twin air conditioned rooms, golf courses - and excellent food.

The England team actually played Argentina twice, with the South Americans treating the games very seriously. They were on the equivalent of £150 a man for a win or draw. Three practice games were also played behind closed doors.

The first full International was to be played on Sunday 17th May, but on the Thursday before, an England XI played an Argentine XI. Tommy put on the white shirt of England for the first time in what was virtually a reserve team and the visitors lost the game 3-1. In the sweltering heat the opposition were superior in all departments, and there was an unbelievable near 100,000 crowd cheering the home side on. Tommy spearheaded the English attack but unfortunately he had no support up front and he was even denied a penalty after he was fouled. However, from a Jack Froggart corner, against the run of play, Tommy scored a great goal with a typical header.

14th May 1953.
Tommy (bottom left) in his first England shirt, at The River Plate Stadium.

In action (in the white shirt), versus Argentina

The next match was a full International played at the River Plate Stadium. However, after 22 minutes of play the game was abandoned due to a torrential downpour with no score. Efforts were made by the English delegation and the Argentine authorities for the game to be played again but they couldn't come to any agreement as regards to a date. For the record Tommy that day played alongside Jimmy Dickinson, Alf Ramsey, Gil Merrick, Billy Wright, Bill Eckersley, Harry Johnstone, Tom Finney, Ivor Broadis, Johnny Berry and Nat Lofthouse. Despite the game lasting only 22 minutes, Tommy was still awarded his first cap.

The following Tuesday the team flew to Chile for a game against the National side. This was England's first ever International match in Chile, and 80,000 spectators saw England win the game 2-1. All the games were refereed by Englishman Arthur Ellis, who for this game had to delay the kick-off by 25 minutes due to many fans who were perched on the roof of the stand. Tommy scored the first goal and Lofthouse the second. The game was significant for Tommy, as in the Chilean line-up were former Oakwell heroes George and Ted Robledo.

On Wednesday the party flew out for a game against the then current World Champions, Uruguay. This was undoubtedly the best game of the tour. The British players were very tired from their trip and twice the plane flew over

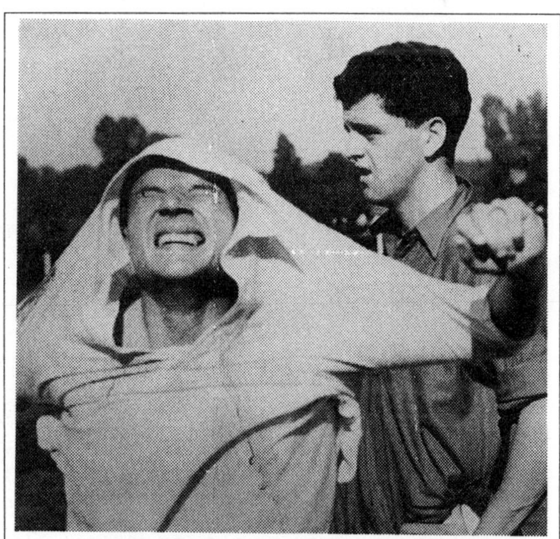

A lighthearted moment during training, John Berry gets in a tangle

Montevideo without being able to land. For the whole 90 minutes of the match, both teams played first class football in the Centenario Stadium. The Uruguians scored after 26 minutes and in the second half scored again after 15 minutes. England netted their only goal, thanks to Tommy, minutes from time. Although England lost it was still considered a good performance. Tommy didn't play in the remaining fixture, against the U.S.A. in the Yankee Stadium, which England won comfortably six goals to three.

He had enjoyed the tour very much and for a young twenty-one year old it was a great experience. Although the tour itself wasn't considered a great success by the press back home, the youngster's performances proved to be one of the high points.

The team arrived back in England on Tuesday 9th June and for Tommy all he wanted to do was to get back home to drop his suitcase off at his mother's, and catch the first bus to Bradford to catch up with Harry England and Bob McCormick, who were on holiday there at the time. With the rest of the summer remaining free he had plenty of time to tell his friends back home in Smithies all about his adventures, which included being introduced to President Peron in Argentina, seeing Cary Grant, and climbing to the top of the Empire State Building in New York.

It's interesting to note that all the time he was playing for United and England not once did he ever boast to anybody about his exploits on the field. Every time he returned home he only spoke about football on very rare occasions, for he just wanted to relax and enjoy himself.

At this time Tommy was courting a girl back home in Barnsley named Norma Curtis. She was the first real girlfriend he ever had. She remembers that time with both happiness and a certain amount of bitterness. Norma recalls: *"The first time I ever saw him was when he was sitting in the street with his leg in plaster. My best friend lived opposite him in St. Helens Avenue and I lived in nearby Belmont Avenue. Later on I used to see him occasionally around town, and he regularly came into this cafe where I was working, with a couple of other Barnsley players such as Doug Kelly and Norman Smith. One night I was on my way home from work and he jumped on the same bus as me and got off at my stop, started talking, and that's how it all began really.*

We did all the things courting couples did then, like go to the pictures and sometimes we'd go off to watch Charlie Williams, who did a club turn then as well as playing for Doncaster Rovers. I remember when he was a kid he used to borrow my brother Donald's boots so he could play for the school team.

I'll never forget the time there was all the talk about the transfer, we were hounded everywhere we went, and they even hung around outside my front door day and night trying to get information from me.

I went up to Manchester with him a couple of days before he played his first game and we were met off the train by Jimmy Murphy, he was a lovely bloke and he gave us a tour around Old Trafford. After Tommy played his first game we travelled back to Barnsley together.

When he was at Barnsley, after the game he hardly ever went home, so he came to my house and I would darn his socks or sew a button on his shirt and give him his tea. We often spoke about money and he said that when he finished playing he would buy a little sports shop, so he knew he couldn't go on playing forever. To be honest he never had any money sense, he never seemed to have any on him at all and I think people bled him dry. At least while he was going out with me I got him to save a few hundred pounds.

Just before he went to South America he asked me to marry him, but I said no because I was only seventeen at the time you see, so we both decided to wait until I was eighteen. At United all the wives and girlfriends went to the home matches and the club provided us with digs. Tommy stayed at Mrs. Watson's, and I stayed at her daughter's. I was particularly friendly with the girlfriends of Colin Webster and David Pegg.

Towards the end people began to get very jealous and they started putting the poison down which eventually led us to splitting up. Basically what happened was that when he went to South America he asked me to go to Manchester to see him off but I couldn't go because I had to get up for work in the morning, so we agreed to write to each other and we said our goodbyes. He wrote every day and I wrote back but the trouble was that by the time he received my letters he had moved on, so

Happier days, in 1952, with girlfriend Norma.

God knows what he thought. Just before he was due back home he sent a telegram to his family saying he would be home on the Tuesday evening, but when I went to see him they said he would be home on Wednesday, and of course he was upset when I wasn't there to greet him. Plus someone had told him that they had seen me in town with another fella, but I was only catching the last bus home from babysitting. I went around to Harry England's and we had a row and that was that. Now you must understand that I wouldn't do anything to hurt that lad, I absolutely idolised him. I found out years later that he eventually found out the truth but it was too late. Looking back I suppose if I had married him I would have been a very young widow, but I have never forgotten our time together."

During May 1953 a popular weekly football magazine, Raich Carter's 'Soccer Star', voted Tommy as most promising newcomer. It was a runaway victory and he took the lead from the very start, finally winning by over a hundred votes. His nearest rivals were Albert Quixall, Jeff Hall, Johnny Haynes and Ron Flowers. The following year also saw him writing a regular column in the popular 'Sports' magazine.

The beginning of the 1953-54 season saw Tommy in his familiar No.9 jersey. He scored his first goal of the season in his second game against Liverpool at Anfield, which ended up in a thrilling four-all draw. By the time the team played Huddersfield in late October, a game which most people now regard as the Busby Babes first League game, Duncan Edwards, Dennis Viollet, Jeff Whitefoot and Jackie Blanchflower were all first team regulars.

On November 3rd 1953, Tommy played for the Football Association against the Army at Hillsborough, Sheffield. In the side that day was team mate Dennis Viollet, as well as Jimmy Meadows, Ron Flowers, Ronnie Allen and Colin Grainger, while included in the opposition were John Charles, Albert Quixall and Alan Finney. It's interesting to note that the opposing centre-forward that day was former Raley pupil, Joe Bonson, who was on Wolves books at the time.

On the 21st of that month Tommy scored his first ever hat-trick for United, against Blackpool at Old Trafford. The match was billed in one National paper as the Giants verses the Babes, and in the all-Lancashire clash United monopolised much of the early play. Tommy was unlucky not to get on the scoresheet as early as the 11th minute, but it was South African Bill Perry, who opened the scoring in the 21st, before Tommy equalised with a header following a lob from Jack Rowley six minutes later.

Five minutes from the interval Viollet netted to make the score 2-1. Tommy went on to score two more goals, to secure a memorable hat-trick. It was indeed a great victory for the United team. Northern sports writer Kevin Wade wrote at the time *"Matt Busby, Manchester United's manager must be a very happy man after his side eclipsed Blackpool yesterday. He saw his babes (seven of his side are 21 or under) turn on another dazzling display that stamps them as stars in the making. This side has been together for four consecutive matches and the 4-1 victory over Blackpool emphasises their new found form. The Busby Boys are here to stay. Chief architect of United's attack was Centre Forward Tommy Taylor. He scored three goals and led the United attack in raid after raid. On this form he looked a better prospect than Stan Mortensen who is playing in Wednesday's International."*

The International which Kevin Wade was referring to was the game against Hungary on the 25th November, 1953. Four of the Blackpool squad played that day, namely Ernie Taylor, Stan Matthews, Harry Johnstone and Stan Mortensen. The game has since gone down in football history, for the invincible - at Wembley - England were beaten 6-3, the first time they had lost to a foreign team on English soil. The speedy, fluent Hungarians gave a display that would have shattered any side. England, ill-prepared - possibly over confident after so many undefeated years - were not in the same class. Not that the England team played badly, in fact their first two goals were taken brilliantly. *"No European Nation has beaten us here and none ever will."* that was your average stubborn Englishman's view before the game. The Hungarians were virtually unknown and the press had almost ignored them, for England were expected to win comfortably, but as soon as Hidegkuti slashed a twenty yard rising shot beyond Merrick in the first minute, the visitors were out to deliver a lesson in accuracy, ball control, moving into position, and finishing.

As a result, six International careers ended that day and Tommy sat at Mrs. Watson's watching the game on television, wondering if he would ever be capped for his country again.

By Christmas 1953, Tommy was playing well and scoring plenty of goals. After the Blackpool game he netted against Portsmouth, and although the team played badly he managed to snatch a late equaliser, a goal which was made possible by League debutant Colin Webster. Tommy scored two more against Liverpool on Christmas day, with his second hat-trick coming in the following game versus Sheffield Wednesday. Two games later however, United were out of the F.A. Cup, beaten in the third round by Burnley at Turf Moor. Such was the impression he made on the First Division that season, many were asking why he wasn't in the England side.

Bob Ferrier, sports writer for the Daily Mirror labled Taylor the forgotten man of English football. He wrote *"In this young footballer you will find the best of Lofthouse and Allen, currently the two 'name' players in the England centre-forward position. He has the strength and speed of the Bolton man and the quickness and skill of the Albion man. He has great talent and power in the air with that suspended float that featured in Lawton's play, and he does it all with splendid spirit and malice to none."* He wrote that piece after watching United's 1-0 victory over Wolves in early March, when Tommy outplayed the great Billy Wright.

On March 27th at Highbury, United lost 3-1 to Arsenal. Henry Rose wrote the following day *"What a pity Taylor, the 22 year-old centre forward had to be on the losing side at Highbury. No one worked harder for victory than Taylor did. He was the outstanding star of this match and showed he could shoot, produce imaginative football and make openings. He opened the scoring with a fine goal in the second minute. United were swamped, young Taylor excepted, and he remained prominent until the end as he chased every goal chance with boundless enthusiasm."* However, the game was marred for Tommy as he picked up an ankle injury which would see him missing the remaining six games of the season. The only other game he had missed that season was the home match against Middlesbrough, way back in September.

The ankle injury proved to be quite serious and at one point, put his playing career into serious doubt. He went into hospital and following a small operation at the end of March he was passed fit by early May, although his ankle was to give him more problems later that summer.

In his first full season playing for the club he was top scorer with 22 goals in 35 appearances, nearly double his nearest rival - his close friend Jackie Blanchflower - with 13. The team had finished higher in the League that season by finishing fourth.

Manchester United 1953/54 season - Tommy's first team group picture
(Back): McNulty, Aston, Chilton, Crompton, Jones, Lewis, Byrne and Gibson.
(Front): Berry, Rowley, Taylor, Pearson, Pegg and Cockburn.

Despite picking up the ankle injury late in the season Tommy was still selected to travel with the England party to the 1954 World Cup games in Switzerland. England played their first group four game against Belgium in Basle, on 17th June, which resulted in a 4-4 draw. In a game played at a furious pace in sweltering conditions, the game went into extra time. At one point, England were leading 3-1 with only 15 minutes remaining.

Tommy received some fair praise for his performance after making some clever runs from the halfway line and creating chances. The only criticisms were that he and Lofthouse, who was centre-forward - while Tommy played at inside-right - each hesitated when they should have had a shot at goal. The press back home thought it was a game the England team should have won, and but for an own goal from Jimmy Dickinson, they would have done so. It proved to be a tiring match, and many players, including Tommy, had to be treated for cramp afterwards.

The next game was against the host Nation, Switzerland. This was an all round better performance. The forward line was re-shuffled as Lofthouse had a sore throat and Stanley Matthews had a toe injury. England won the match 2-0, thanks to goals from Jimmy Mullen and Dennis Wilshaw. Tommy played well and it was the first time he had ever led the English attack. He showed some neat touches and nearly scored when his shot went inches over the bar in the second half.

Reporting from Berne the following day, Charles Buchan wrote: *"Young Tommy Taylor leading the attack - his proper place - had the Swiss defenders worried by his pace and ball control. He earned at least one goal."*

In the draw for the Quarter finals, England faced the holders Uruguay. However, they lost the game 4-2. Tommy wasn't picked to play in this match because Nat Lofthouse was fit and Tommy's ankle had started giving him some trouble. The tournament was won by West Germany who had beaten the fancied Hungarians by three goals to two.

The following 1954-55 season didn't start too well for Tommy at all. During Christmas, following a dispute back at Mrs. Watson's, he moved houses. After a short stay in a house in Arlington Road, Stretford, he moved to number 22 Great Stone, to live with Mrs. Swinchat and her family.

Tommy missed the first four games of the season due to his nagging ankle injury, which caused him some trouble for several months. It was expected that all would be well after the operation, but the problem persisted. With nobody believing him, it was thought at one time that Tommy was trying to 'pull the wool' over Busby's eyes, but eventually a specialist found a piece of floating bone, and he went on to make a full recovery. During Tommy's absence, Colin Webster was an able deputy and Dennis Viollet was scoring goals, netting five in four matches. Tommy returned for the home game against Charlton on 4th September, and scored one goal, but then missed the following two matches. It was an uphill struggle since the operation and it took a while before his old form returned. Someone had to pay for Tommy's enforced lay off and the unlucky man was Cardiff City's goalkeeper, Ron Howells. The Welsh side received a 5-2 trouncing at Old Trafford with Tommy scoring four.

United's quest for F.A. Cup glory began against Reading where they came out eventual 4-1 winners after a replay. Tommy didn't play as he had picked up an injury during a practice match. In the fourth round they faced Manchester City in a local derby, but Tommy, on his 23rd birthday, failed to score and United lost 2-0. Of the 42 games played that season Tommy had missed 12. The season proved to be a very frustrating one for him, but despite the injuries he still managed to be United's top goal scorer with 20.

The summer saw team mates Roger Byrne and Duncan Edwards go with the England party for a three match tour abroad. The team played Portugal, Spain and France, losing two and drawing one. The tour was disappointing and it seemed the England selectors had lost faith in Tommy, picking Nat Lofthouse and Dennis Wilshaw as their forwards. Tommy wouldn't play for his country again for another eleven months.

Albert Scanlon gives a brief insight into life at Old Trafford during the mid-fifties and recalls one or two of the funnier moments he shared with Tommy. *"I suppose you have to respect Murphy's judgement, he certainly picked a good'un when he saw Tommy. You had the centre-forwards of that era, like Trevor Ford, Roy Bentley, plus Nat Lofthouse. Then all of a sudden you had this young fellow who would run from one end of the pitch to the other, six foot, slim and well built and he was going past people, laying-off balls which wasn't the norm then.*

If you talk to the old-time supporters they'll talk about Duncan, Roger and Eddie and then they'll talk about Tommy. The nearest they've ever got to him in the last thirty odd years are David Herd and Mark Hughes. They took some terrible knocks but they always got up and went again.

Taylor ran the forward line at Old Trafford alongside the likes of Johnny Berry, Dennis Viollet, David Pegg and Billy Whelan. Billy could always find him and the winger's job was to get the ball into the box as they knew Tommy would be there. If you could ever get a video of all the goals Dennis Viollet scored for United, many would be ricochets and rebounds, thanks to the havoc caused by Tommy in the penalty area. He got through a tremendous amount of work from the halfway line and defenders weren't used to big forwards going past them.

Back in the fifties the tactics and training wasn't like it is today We always had Mondays off and we'd all go off to Davyhulme Golf Club, and although Tommy was usually right handed, for golf and cricket he always used his left hand. I never played golf at all and I only went for the dinner. On the Tuesday we would all have a practice match and all Wednesday was were some laps and a good workout in the Gym. Thursday was more laps and then a game of five a side.

It sounds daft talking about it now but Manchester in the fifties had some terrible fogs and as grown men we would split into two groups and go off and play hide and seek, it's funny how you remember little things like that. All Friday consisted of were some sprints and a team talk, Matt with the first team and Jimmy with the reserves. I've said this many times before, but the pair of them could reel off every single player in the First Division and we always knew by Friday dinnertime who was playing.

I remember a fellow wrote to me once asking if I could bring Tommy along to a New Years Eve Dance. He had tickets for Belle Vue and at first he wouldn't go but I managed to persuade him in the end. I promised him a good time but when we got there it was the school hall in Kersley and Tommy was gutted because there was no drink and no women. He actually carried a card around in his wallet which read 'The Worlds' Greatest Beer Drinker'. To his credit though, he still managed to walk around and be polite to people and I spent the rest of the evening apologising in the pub across the road. Tommy and Jackie were great pals and they could never pass Belle Vue without going in. He fell in love with the place but I suppose they never had anything like that back in Barnsley. There was a zoo, dance halls, wrestling and a speedway track.

Being with him was fun. I roomed with him on our end of season tour to Denmark and all I can say is that it was a real education. He went missing for nearly two days and nobody knew where he had gone. Tom Curry asked me where he was and I said I didn't know. What had happened was that he had gone to this club, and I must say that Tommy attracted people like flies, and he had gone off with this woman. He strolled in one morning and I said, 'bleedin hell where have you been, Tosher's been looking for you', and all he could say was that it was 'brilliant, really brilliant'. Anyway, we went down to breakfast and sat down at this long table, but what had happened was that, although I didn't know it at the time, Busby had a cold and was bedridden for two days. This particular morning, he was seated at the top with Mr. Gibson, Bill Inglis and Tom Curry and everyone thought Tommy would get a right rollicking. But he just came down, sat down, looked up and said 'alright boss, not seen you for a couple of days, where've you been?' You should have seen the sweat on Tom Curry's face.

Another incident which sticks out in my mind about the trip to Denmark is that some sailors wrote to Busby asking him for tickets for the game and he obliged. Anyhow after the game, me, Tommy, Mark and David got invited back to one of the ships for some dinner. In return David had asked the Captain if some of the sailors could come out for a drink with us and he said yes as long as we got them back at a reasonable hour. So we went into this club one dinnertime which was open twenty-four hours a day, but Mark wasn't too bothered so he went off to the zoo. I must admit that I wasn't a big drinker and two lagers made me sick. The lads kept drinking but the time was flying by and I kept looking at my watch and saying we gotta go because we were going to a do that night, which had been arranged by the Danish Football Association, in Tiverley Gardens. In the end Tommy ended up dancing with the proprietor's wife so I phoned a couple of taxis to take us to the docks to drop the sailors off. Everybody had had a good drink. When we got there the Captain came down the gang plank and it was obvious to see the sailors were in serious trouble. All of a sudden, the door to the first taxi opened and Tommy fell out. There was a little bit of a scuffle and two Danish Policemen came over with long sticks and were about to hit him when the Captain intervened and explained that this was the England centre-forward.

I got him back to the hotel as quickly as possible and told Tom Curry. Later that evening, he turned up at Tiverley Gardens laughing, joking, sober as a judge looking immaculate in his suit as if nothing had happened. He could be a real character at times."

Not many people had predicted championship honours in the 1955-56 season for United. Most thought the side contained too many youngsters and lacked experience. The team was just considered an exciting prospect for the future. Certainly the season didn't start off too promising at all with the team only winning three games from the first eight.

In the opening fixture against Birmingham City, Tommy was injured during the first half. He moved onto the wing and Colin Webster moved to centre-forward, remaining on the pitch for the rest of the game but with little or no effect. He missed the next seven games but came back to score his first goal of the season in a 3-2 win over Preston on September 17th. However, his old form soon returned and in between the Preston game and United getting knocked out of the Cup against Bristol Rovers in early January, Tommy had scored fourteen goals. He reached a milestone in his career at Old Trafford when he scored in his 100th League appearance, against Burnley on February 4th, 1956.

Frank Swift wrote after watching the game: *"On a skating rink of a pitch, Taylor stood out like a Cortina gold medalist, mastering the conditions and the lively ball with an ease that defied the laws of equilibrium. He had an uncanny knack of being in a good position, unmarked. He had two near misses in the first half but just after the start of the second he snapped up a loose clearance in the centre circle. He beat one man, veered left, evaded another and as two defenders came in on him he let fly with a great right-footer that whizzed past the keeper from 18 yards."*

A few weeks later saw Tommy selected to play for England 'B' against Scotland 'B' at Dundee. The game was a poor one and England were expected to win with ease, but they found themselves 2-1 down. To their credit, however, they continued to press forward and with barely three minutes to go Tommy scored the equaliser. Man of the match, scoring one goal, making another, two headers just over the bar and two shots brilliantly saved he did everything that really mattered and was England's outstanding player.

His only other game for England 'B' was against the Switzerland 'B' team at Southampton in late March. Playing alongside team-mates David Pegg and Duncan Edwards, he scored a hat-trick as England went on to win 4-1.

Manchester United had virtually secured the League title by Christmas having gone top they never looked back. They lost only once between January 1st and the end of the season, going on to win the Championship by the then record of eleven points. On April 7th a post war record crowd of 62,277 packed Old Trafford to watch the Busby Babes formally claim the title by beating Blackpool 2-1.

A joke is shared at the Championship reception. (left to right), Frank Swift, David Pegg, Tommy Taylor and Mark Jones. All four were to lose their lives at Munich.

Matt Busby wasn't present at the game, he was attending a funeral in Glasgow and left to return to Manchester just as the game was about to start. After 'phoning from Abington, he was told his team were a goal down, He 'phoned again from Lockerbie and discovered his side were winning 2-1. There were no more telephone calls until full time. When he arrived back in Manchester he had special praise for Tommy who had scored the winner 10 minutes from time, and once again he was top goalscorer, netting 25 from 33 appearances.

The championship reception was held at the Town Hall on the Saturday evening following the last game of the season against Portsmouth. Over 450 representatives of the City's sporting community and the Mayor came to honour the club. More than 3,000 fans cheered the arrival of the team bus in Albert Square, and a specially erected platform was built over the Town Hall steps. First to make a speech was Mayor Alderman Tom Regan, followed by captain Roger Byrne. The crowd then shouted for Tommy to make a speech. This is something he found very difficult and all he could manage to say was: *"Thank you on behalf of myself and my team mates."* Later he bought himself a book called 'Teach Yourself Public Speaking' in a bid to better himself.

The Championship was a great achievement but no one could have predicted what was to follow the next season. Before the new season (1956-57) commenced, Tommy went on to gain another five caps including his first home International, at Hampden Park against Scotland. He missed United's last but one League game against Sunderland, and instead appeared against a Scottish side which hadn't beaten England at Hampden since 1937. The Scots faced a two pronged attack down the middle from Taylor and Lofthouse. It was Tommy's sixth cap and he was once again asked to masquerade as a goal poaching inside-right. For the fifth time in six games for England he was playing out of position and out of character as assistant to Lofthouse. It appeared that he was the victim of the selectors religious devotion to the twin centre forward-system which most people regarded as no system at all. Many were saying that this system should be scrapped because it wasn't working, and a new forward line up should be present at Wembley in May for the game against Brazil. At the Scotland game England scored an equaliser less than 30 seconds from time, thanks to Johnny Haynes, and managed to scrape a 1-1 draw. Tommy though was to find himself as the number one choice by the end of 1956 for the centre-forward position.

Before the Brazil game, Barnsley played an All Star XI, a team which comprised mainly ex-Oakwell players, the aim was to raise money for the Barnsley players Benefit Fund. The previous day Tommy was in Belfast playing for the Football League against the Irish League and the Barnsley match was his fourth game in ten days. He was made Captain for the night, and in his team he had former Oakwell favourites, Jimmy Baxter, Gavin Smith, Cecil McCormack, Eddie McMorran, Johnny Kelly, United team-mate Mark Jones, Danny Blanchflower, and Sam Bartram who had assisted the side during the war. This makeshift team won buy six goals to nil.

May 9th saw the visit of Brazil to Wembley. The South Americans were on a 7 match tour of Europe and had lost only once, against Italy in Milan. It was a memorable game and just the tonic English football needed. Tommy scored twice, as did Colin Grainger, with the end result being 4-2. It should have been six but Roger Byrne and John Atyeo missed a penalty each. Cliff Webb reported in the Daily Herald the following day *"This was superb England stuff, with Edwards and Taylor shattering the opposition with clear cut skill and swiftness of movement and the whole team clicking like clockwork."* It was an encouraging result for manager Walter Winterbottom whose side was due to embark on a three match tour of the Continent that very same month.

(Right) Tommy makes another goal challenge - this time it's in the Brazil match.

(Below)
The England team line-up, before the match with West Germany, May 1956.
(From left): Byrne, Matthews, Edwards, Grainger, Hall, Haynes, Astall, Taylor, Clayton, Wilshaw and Wright.

The first match on the tour against Sweden saw a fairly poor performance by virtually the whole team. True the strong winds, glaring sunshine and a bumpy pitch didn't help but the team were expected to come away with something better than a 0-0 result. It wouldn't be dismissed as a total disappointment, as England were still trying to weld together a new young side for the next World Cup.

Next came Finland where three goals in thirteen minutes made victory a certainty. Again it was by no means a vintage England performance but they were far superior than the amateur Finns. Before the game Tommy had pre-match injections for a boil on his arm and just before half-time, following a collision with the Finnish goalkeeper Hurri, he signalled to the bench that he couldn't go on and was replaced by Nat Lofthouse who went on to score two goals to break Steve Bloomer's 45 year old record of International 29 goals. The game ended in a 5-1 victory, and its also interesting to note that as well as Roger Byrne and Duncan Edwards in the England line-up that day, Tommy also had in the eleven fellow team- mate Ray Wood keeping goal.

Although Tommy was doubtful for the final game against the current World champions West Germany on May 26th, he was passed fit and he played a key part in what was a great win for the England side. Goals from Johnny Haynes, Colin Grainger plus a memorable effort from Duncan Edwards gave the team a 3-1 win in a match which finished the tour in style.

Manchester United, since the heady days of the 1950's, have gone on to win more League championships, F.A. Cups and even capturing the European Cup (in 1968), but in the 1956/57 season, they were on the brink of a unique treble, and although in the end they went on to win just one of the possible three trophies on offer, that season saw them embark on a journey that was to make them a household name both in this country and across Europe.

They defended the League title in great style losing only once between the first game - at home against Birmingham City in August - and November 10th, when they lost to Bolton. Up to the New Year Tommy had scored fourteen goals and he missed only two games, those versus Portsmouth and Charlton. The Charlton game was missed due to another appearance for England in a home International against Northern Ireland at Windsor Park, Belfast. The game ending up a one-all draw with, England's goal being scored by Stanley Matthews.

By January 1957 United were four points clear at the top of the table, and in all honesty there was never any doubt about who would win the title. On into the New Year and the team lost only three more matches before the end of the campaign. In the League that season Tommy played 32 matches scoring 22 goals. Billy Whelan was top marksman with 26, but he had played seven more games.

With United having won the Championship the previous season, they were invited to take part in the European Cup, and against the wishes of the Football Association they accepted, thus being the first English side to enter the competition. In September United travelled to Belgium to play Anderlecht in the Preliminary Round 1st leg game. Tommy and Dennis Viollet got a goal a piece for a 2-0 win.

What followed at Maine Road a couple of weeks later made the world sit up and take notice of this gifted young side. On a magical rainy night in Manchester, England's champions were in tremendous form as they beat Anderlecht 10-0, a record score in this competition. No team could have lived with United that night. Viollet scored four, Whelan two, one from Berry and a hat-trick from Tommy - who in fact started the rout as early as the 8th minute.

In the second round United had a tougher time against West German champions Borussia Dortmund, having won the first leg by three goals to two they hung on to a goalless draw in Germany to go through on aggregate.

The quarter final games against Athletico Bilbao were arguably the greatest matches the Busby Babes ever played. They were drawn away in the first leg and in very poor conditions United were soon trailing by three

Tommy and an Anderlecht player in good spirits at the after-match Banquet. But there was only one player smiling after the second leg!

goals. People say great goalscorers hunt in pairs and that definitely applied to Tommy Taylor and Dennis Viollet, who scored one a piece to bring the deficit back to 3-2. Then Bilbao regained the lead with two silly goals to make it 5-2, and United looked down and out, until a great goal from Irishman Billy Whelan gave the side a glimmer of hope. It was a tall order to expect United to win the return by three clear goals, but not impossible. On a night of great excitement Tommy played like a man inspired. First a goal from Viollet and then one from Tommy, could they score just one more? In a nail-biting finale, and despite having two goals disallowed, 70,000 fans cheered and clapped as Tommy set up the dramatic winner for Johnny Berry to score that elusive third under the Maine Road floodlights, and hence go through 6-5 on aggregate.

The following day, George Follows wrote of Taylor *"My heart still beats like a Tom-Tom, as I endeavour to describe the greatest match I ever saw, which was cheered by the greatest crowd I ever heard and starred the greatest centre-forward exhibition I ever saw. It was Tommy Taylor's game and the game of Tommy Taylor's lifetime. But Manchester United, led by the six foot and thirteen stone of fighting fury that was Taylor, just gobbled them up on their way to the semi-finals of the European Cup."* They now faced the mighty Real Madrid who had won the first competition the year before.

The week before the earlier Anderlecht game saw the lad from Barnsley playing for the Football League in Dublin against the League of Ireland. It ended in a three-all draw with Tommy netting one of the goals. Before United started their quest for F.A. Cup glory in January, Tommy had won himself two more caps.

The first came against Yugoslavia at Wembley on 28th November and was a friendly match. The Yugoslav team were a good side who had never lost to England, and many people saw the game as a pointer to England's World Cup prospects. Tommy was a substitute for this game and he wasn't even mentioned in the match programme. Although substitutes weren't permitted in domestic football at this time, for International matches a replacement - up to the 44th minute - was allowed, although the goalkeeper could be changed at any time during the game. However, a first half injury to Johnny Haynes saw Tommy come on and score two goals to help the side to a 3-0 win.

His second England appearance was in the preliminary round of the World Cup against Denmark on December 5th at Wolverhampton Wanderers ground, Molineux. It was to be a great night for the United pair of Taylor and Edwards, with the latter grabbing two goals and Tommy scoring a superb hat-trick to earn a 5-2 victory. It was after this game that Henry Rose, sportswriter for the Daily Express, caused a minor sensation when he wrote in his column that.... *"If Tommy Taylor was England's best centre-forward then I'm Santa Claus."* He basically accused Tommy of not being in top form after seeing him miss some chances during the match. It seemed a rather harsh statement at the time, for if you scored a hat-trick against class opposition today, you would be a National hero! Criticism is something Tommy took in his stride, for he realised that as a centre-forward, people looked upon you to score goals and win matches. Whereas if you had a bad game, the fans and the press weren't slow in letting you know how they felt. Anyhow the Henry Rose column the following week carried the headline: *"All Right I'm Santa....it's your verdict"*, and he went on to say *"Your verdict is loud and clear, I am Santa Claus. An avalanche of abuse and unseasonable ill-will descended on me following my criticism of the Manchester United centre-forward in my match report. It is impossible to print all the printable abuse."*

United's attempt for F.A. Cup glory began away to Hartlepool on 3rd January, where they managed to win 4-3 with Tommy scoring one of the goals. He then netted two more in the fourth round game against Wrexham as United came away comfortable 5-0 winners. Round 5 saw the visit of Everton to Old Trafford and it was Tommy's first ever home cup-tie. The last time United were drawn at home was against London amateurs Walthamstow Avenue in January 1953. The United team were a bit worried as Everton had whacked them 5-2 in the League earlier in the season. However, they needn't have worried, as a Duncan Edwards goal ensured the teams' passage through to the next round.

With the second successive championship virtually in the bag, the team was progressing well in the Cup with a quarter-final tie versus Bournemouth a few weeks away, and also their European Cup semi-final game against Real Madrid to look forward to. Unfortunately Tommy suffered another aggravating injury to spoil his otherwise great season.

He was hurt in a match against Charlton on 18th February, which left him wincing after a heavy tackle. He left the field for a few minutes to receive treatment, but returned to score twice. He lined up for the following game against Blackpool, but after a matter of minutes he began to feel the effects of this injury and spent most of the first half limping on the wing. He began the second half at outside-right but limped off after ten minutes. A cracked shin bone was diagnosed and the pain stretched from his knee to his ankle.

It put him out of both the games against Bournemouth, plus the semi- final with Birmingham City at Hillsborough, and also the next five League games. United beat Bournemouth and in the semi-final, they overcame Birmingham 2-0. So with Wembley and a European Cup semi-final not too far away it was a race against time for Tommy to get fit for these two important games.

In the first week of April, Matt, Jimmy and Bert Whalley travelled to the Baseball ground for a mid-week Central League game against Derby reserves. It was Tommy's first full 90 minutes since the injury and what a way to return, for on a very icey pitch he scored a superb hat-trick. His first League game back was in the goalless draw with Spurs, and although he was rusty and missed some good chances, he was just glad to be back in the first team again. April 12th brought United their semi-final date with Madrid. 125,000 spectators - no doubt the largest crowd ever to watch United - were packed into the Bernabeu Stadium for the game.

Left to contemplate his football return, following his injury. March 1957.

No British team had ever experienced a situation like this before, but sadly United lost 3-1. George Follows headline in the Daily Herald wrote: *"Murder in Madrid"* and he went on to write *"Centre-half Marquitos justified his reputation as the champion clogger of Spain. He slashed Tommy Taylor off at the stocking tops in the 18th minute. He nudged, jostled or obstructed him at every opportunity."* Follows certainly had no praise at all for referee Leo Horn and claimed that he should have sent off De Stefano following a vicious sliding tackle on Jackie Blanchflower. But Madrid were just too worldly wise for England's young champions. It was Tommy who scored United's only goal, when he rose high to Whelan's centre to head home eight minutes from time. After the game Tommy said *"The first time Marquitos kicked me he caught me right on the spot where I hurt it six weeks ago. I was surprised I walked off the field after this, I thought I was going to be carried off."* The day after flying home it was back to the League fixtures and Tommy scored both of United's goals in the 2-0 victory over Luton Town.

...... But he was even friendlier with the Senorinas!

The return game with Madrid was United's first European Cup match under the new Old Trafford floodlights. Raymond Kopa and De Stefeno scored two goals in the first half and it was obvious United couldn't come back from 5-1 down on aggregate, but to their credit they came out in the second half and scored two goals, thanks to Bobby Charlton and Billy Whelan. Although they couldn't repeat the type of performance that was achieved over Bilbao, it was nethertheless a great experience for the team.

(Above) Real Madrid's goalkeeper Alonso saves from Taylor's shot, in the European Cup match at the Bernabeu Stadium. (Below) Concentration and taut neck muscles, with Manchester City's Trautman poised to save the header, in a local derby match.

With the treble now gone, Matt Busby had his sights set on the double, a feat which no other side had achieved in modern times. The Championship was secured five days before the Madrid match, in the game against Sunderland, with goals from Tommy, Whelan and Edwards. It was Tommy, who scored in the 89th Minute, that clinched it. The points total of 64 was the best in the Division since Arsenal's total of 66 in 1931.

Tommy missed the last three games of the season in a bid to be fit for the Cup Final against Aston Villa. It was a final which United were expected to win, but six minutes into the game - when McParland carelessly charged Ray Wood - quashed this expectation. Jackie Blanchflower went in goal and did well, and with 10 men United held on until half-time. Wood appeared briefly on the right wing in the second-half, but was ineffective, and two goals by Irishman Peter McParland put an end to any dreams United may have had of the double. With ten minutes to go Duncan Edwards took a corner for Tommy to head a great looping header beyond the reach of Villa Keeper, Nigel Sims. He also netted three minutes from time but the 'goal' was disallowed for off-side. A dazed Wood went back in goal but to no avail, and United lost 2-1.

Tommy (2nd player from left) about to be introduced to
H.R.H. The Duke of Edinburgh, at the Cup Final.

It was a disappointing end to a memorable season but the players promised they'd be back next year. Sadly, Tommy and seven of his team-mates wouldn't.

During May 1957 Tommy became the subject of a transfer abroad. Early reports suggested that Real Madrid wanted to pay United £70,000 for his services, and he would have received a £20,000 signing-on fee. At the time Tommy was earning £15 a week at Old Trafford, but the report was merely speculation. The bid from Milan a month later was far more serious.

Milan first approached Busby when the United team were in Copenhagen for their end of season tour, and he turned them down flat. Busby said nothing to Tommy about the approach of the 'Internationale' representative, Lajos Cseisler, and he only found out about the interest in him when he spoke to Archie Ledbrooke. Apparently Cseisler was prepared to offer the same terms that had tempted Leeds United and John Charles - £55,000 for the club and £10,000 for the player.

Matt Busby was in Switzerland in June for a youth tournament when he discovered Milan had approached Tommy behind his back. This made Busby furious and he contacted the F.A. to try and get some kind of International control over these situations. Matt wasn't due back from his trip until 8th June, so towards the end of May he sent Tommy into hiding in Llandudno to keep him away from all the press and speculation. Some schoolboys discovered him playing football on the John Brights Grammar School pitch, but he refused to sign any autographs, and went back into hiding where he waited for Matt's return.

At first the only person to know his whereabouts was Harry England, who at the time had the press knocking on his door offering him money to tell them where he was, but he remained silent. A move abroad never materialised.

Meanwhile back in Manchester, Tommy had met a girl named Carol, who would most certainly have become his wife. His only other girlfriend, around this time, was Ann Sutton, who as well as seeing Tommy was also going out with a rugby player. Apparently she was seen by some people as a kind of 'sports groupie', and worked at the Lancaster Paper Mill along with Matt's daughter Sheena, who at the time was married to Don Gibson. Ann Sutton achieved fame after the 1956 championship, when she was pictured with Tommy drinking champagne from a shoe. On a Sunday Tommy would often go to Longford Park to watch the football, and it was here that he met Carol Philipson, a local girl born and bred in Stretford. They'd sit for hours in the local cafe chatting, and on Christmas Eve 1957 they became engaged.

A thoughtful Tommy
in his Llandudno hideaway - May 1957.

A night out with Fiancee Carol Philipson

By mid-1957, things were looking good for Tommy. Two championship medals, a Cup Final appearance with his club, he was an automatic choice for his country, and with his growing prosperity, he used some of his money to buy a red M.G. Sports car.

In May he played in three Internationals, each of which was a World Cup-tie. The first, on the 8th, was at Wembley against the Republic of Ireland, and in an emphatic 5-1 victory, Tommy had an excellent game scoring his second hat-trick in a full International. Next came the return game with Denmark in Copenhagen, and once again he got on the scoresheet scoring two goals in the team's 4-1 victory. Finally on the 19th of the month, in Dublin, England worked hard for a 1-1 draw in a game which saw David Pegg win his only full cap. With the hard work over and done with England had qualified for the 1958 World Cup in Sweden.

At the start of the 1957/58 season Matt Busby's dream of three consecutive League championships - like Huddersfield and Arsenal in the inter-war years - got off to a good start with five wins and twenty-two goals. Some revenge was also obtained against Aston Villa for the F.A. Cup Final defeat, with a four-nil victory in the F.A. Charity Shield with the ex-Barnsley 'goal machine' netting a hat- trick.

Following a 1-0 defeat against Chelsea at Old Trafford, Busby made some team changes. The side had lost too many silly games, including a 3-0 defeat at Portsmouth, 4-0 at Bolton, but more crucially 3-1 to Wolves who were at the top of the table, and the fans weren't slow in letting Busby know how they felt.

Tommy missed his first game of the season, on October 19th (the Portsmouth match), as he was playing at Ninian Park for the England team against Wales. It was to be his third appearance in a home International. He failed to score but the team came away eventual 4-0 winners thanks to an own goal, plus two from Johnny Haynes and one from Tom Finney. November 6th saw the visit of Northern Ireland to Wembley in what was to be a shock 3-2 defeat for England. It was only the second time Tommy had been on the losing side in all his International matches, and he came in for some mild criticism from the press, with one article saying: *"He is a red devil in the red shirt of United but a white elephant in the white shirt of England."* Again it was probably a bit harsh, as every player is entitled to have an off day. Tommy's partner up front that day was Derek Kevan, who many regarded as raw-boned and clumsy, and certainly not of international class.

The team got back to their winning ways in what transpired to be Tommy's last appearance for England, on November 27th against France at Wembley, when he scored two cracking goals in the 3rd and 33rd minutes, with future England manager Bobby Robson getting the other two for a 4-0 win.

Meanwhile on the domestic front United had found their feet again with players such as Albert Scanlon, Kenny Morgans, plus Bobby Charlton holding first team places, and Ray Wood had given way for new signing Harry Gregg. The team remained unbeaten in seven games up until the end of January, and were in hot pursuit of Wolves who were top. To ensure the beating of Stan Cullis' side United had to win all of their remaining games.

Once again they had their sights set on the European Cup. In September in the preliminary round 1st leg, 45,000 saw United face Shamrock Rovers in Dublin. The reds triumphed 6-0 with Tommy scoring twice. The return at Old Trafford was somewhat embarrassing, as United were lucky to get away with a 3-2 victory. The Czech champions Dukla Prague, United's next opponents, were beaten 3-0 in Manchester in November, with Tommy, Colin Webster and David Pegg getting the goals. A victory which was more than enough to allow for the 1-0 defeat over in Prague in the second leg.

More European opposition came next in the quarter-final when United faced Red Star Belgrade. A 2-1 victory at Old Trafford, thanks to goals from Bobby Charlton and a rare effort from Eddie Colman, gave United a one goal cushion to take to Yugoslavia for the return game to be played in the first week of February.

Meanwhile the F.A. Cup saw victories over Workington and Ipswich, with the team having to face Sheffield Wednesday in the fifth round.

Before the Manchester United party flew out to Yugoslavia to meet Red Star they travelled to London to meet Arsenal at Highbury. In a game which is now regarded as a classic, United shot into a 3-0 lead before half time, with goals from Edwards, Charlton and Tommy, but following a remarkable three minute spell, Arsenal hit a treble to level the scores. The Busby Boys remained calm and never panicked, and once again the partnership of Tommy and Dennis Viollet produced a brace of goals to give United the lead again, before a late goal from Arsenal made the score 5-4. It was a thrilling match that kept the crowd of over 63,000 on their toes for the full 90 minutes.

(Left to right) Tommy Taylor, David Pegg and Roger Byrne
relive the highlights of the Bilbao match

Albert Scanlon remembers the time he became a first team regular and particularly the Arsenal match: *"We never thought we'd get beat, even in the home game against Madrid the lads were extremely confident. They got beat by Chelsea and the boss went out and bought Harry Gregg from Doncaster, stuck Mark Jones back in at centre-half, brought in young Kenny Morgans, Bobby Charlton came back, and I went in for David Pegg, and we went for about ten games in the League and Cup unbeaten. By he way, the players were never dropped at Old Trafford they were always 'rested'.*

We went down to London on the Friday and I went to see Frank Sinatra in the film 'Pal Joey' at Marble Arch, along with Eddie Colman, who was a big Sinatra fan. The cinema was only six or seven minutes away from the Lancaster Gate Hotel where we were staying.

On Friday night one of the directors, George Whittaker, died and it really brought it home to us when we were given black armbands just before the kick-off. In the first half we gave them a right going over, and although they came back and scored to draw level, it never entered my head that we would lose. The stadium was just a bubble of sound and I think we would have beaten anybody that day. Me and Kenny ripped holes out of the full-backs.

The boss wasn't annoyed that we let them put four past us and on the journey back to Manchester the lads were elated. We got off at London Road, and me, Tommy and Jackie went into a club called the Costa, and sitting in the club that evening - although I never took much notice at the time - was Denis Law."

Tommy had a lot to look forward to after the Red Star game. If the team got through, there was a second successive semi-final appearance in the European Cup, they were still in the

F.A. Cup, and the first League game after their return was against Wolves in what many people considered the championship decider. In addition he was England's automatic choice for the centre-forward position and he was looking forward to playing in the World Cup finals in Sweden that summer. He was even planning to be married in June or July. When Tommy packed his bags for the Belgrade trip the future looked very bright indeed.

Best man at the 1956 wedding of Tommy's great friend Jackie Blanchflower

CHAPTER FOUR

THE FINAL WHISTLE

On Monday February 3rd 1958, Tommy met up with Duncan Edwards, Ken Morgans and waved goodbye to his landlady, Mrs. Swinchat. They had to go to Old Trafford where they were due to catch the coach which would then take them to Ringway Airport to start the long journey to Belgrade and the European Cup Quarter Final.

Early fog at the airport had delayed take-off for nearly an hour. The flight took six hours, with a stop at Munich to re-fuel. The Elizabethan aircraft was the only plane to land in Belgrade that day due to bad visibility.

"The thing that stands out in my mind on the day we flew out was that Mark Jones was late for the bus." Albert recalls, *"Tommy and the rest of the lads were in high spirits following the Arsenal game, but the flight out was fairly uneventful. When we re-fuelled at Munich me and Mark bought ourselves a St. Christopher each - little use they were. When we eventually landed we were surrounded by fans and loads of photographers and reporters from all across Europe. Apparently there was talk about the pitch being frozen for Wednesday's match, but we were told not to worry because it would be thawed out in time for the kick off, which was about quarter to three.*

We arrived in Belgrade at Monday tea time and went to this hotel, and for some reason there were armed guards on every floor. We were on the fourth floor so by the time we got our meals they were stone cold. Before we flew out we were told to take plenty of razors, chocolate and toothpaste as it was better than having ready cash.

Anyhow after we unpacked, Tommy, me and a few others went for a walk about, and you may not believe this but there were actually people walking about in shoes made from old car tyres. It was incredible, and in all the shops people had to queue for everything. Tommy found a skating rink which was really a frozen lake and he went on with Jackie. It's a good job they never got injured. On the Tuesday we all went training, even the press team and the aircraft crew came along as well. The pitch was icy but Roger had a good run out and declared himself fit for the game. After training we went to the pictures and the first two rows were cleared for us, and I felt really sorry for the people who had paid good money to watch the film, although they couldn't understand it anyway because it was all in English. On the whole though Belgrade was a dismal place with not much to do and nowhere to go".

The match had caught the imagination of the Belgrade public, for as the team boarded the coach on Wednesday to take them to the stadium they passed hundreds of singing, chanting football fans. At the ground the terraces were packed with thousands of swaying, excited soccer fans who were anticipating a great game.

KUP EVROPSKIH FUTBALSKIH ŠAMPIONA

„Manchester united"

Poslednji red (s leva na desno): Eddie *Colman*, Wilf Mc*Guinness*, Colin *Webster*, Ray *Wood*, David *Pegg*, Dennis *Viollet*, Johnny *Berry*; (Srednji red): Tom *Curry* (trener), Jackie *Blanchflower*, Tommy *Taylor*, Fred *Goodwin*, Mark *Jones*, Duncan *Edwards*, Bill *Whelan*, Bill *Foulkes*, Matt *Busby* (menadžer); (Sede): Walter *Grickmer* (sekretar), G. E. *Whittaker* (direktor), H. P. *Hardman* (vođa ekipe), Roger *Byrne* (kapiten), W. H. *Petherbridge* (direktor), J. A. *Gibson* (direktor).

„Crvena zvezda"

5-II-1958

Stadion JNA   **Početak u 14.45**

Cena din. 30.—

They weren't to be disappointed for the game itself had everything, goals, disputed decisions, frcc kicks and fouls, all in a game that was played at a furious pace.

Although he never got on the scoresheet, Tommy played his heart out that afternoon and was responsible for United's first goal. He gathered a clearance in his own half following an unsuccessful raid in the United area, and moved gracefully towards the Red Star goal along with Dennis Viollet. With the Red Star defence spreadeagled, rather than shoot himself, he unselfishly laid the ball to Dennis, who was in a better position to put the ball past goalkeeper Beara. Bobby Charlton scored the second after twenty minutes and he also netted the third.

The team appeared to be on their way to a comfortable victory, but they were unaware of the gallant fightback the Red Star team were about to make. Two minutes after the break, Tommy's great friend Sekularac pulled one back, and following a perfectly good tackle on Zebec by Billy Foulkes, the players were stunned when the referee pointed to the Penalty spot. Tasic scored to make it 3-2, surely United could hang on. Then Harry Gregg allegedly handled the ball outside his penalty area. Red Star were awarded a free kick and Kostic duly scored to make it level. United, with their backs to the wall, managed to hold on until the final whistle to go through to the next round 5-4 on aggregate.

The last team line-up of the Busby Babes - 5 February 1958
(From left): Duncan Edwards, Eddie Colman, Mark Jones, Ken Morgans, Bobby Charlton,
Dennis Viollet, Tommy Taylor, Bill Foulkes, Harry Gregg, Albert Scanlon, Roger Byrne

It was a great win for the team and it was a great relief to get through the ordeal. In the evening the players went to a banquet at the British Embassy and each member of the team was presented with a tea set and a bottle of gin. Everyone was in a good mood and Matt even allowed his players to go to a nightclub if they wished.

Some of the players and members of the press team went to a club called 'The Crystal', where they were entertained by various dancing and cabaret acts. Tommy had gone to the club and he left about 1.00am., and made his way back to the Hotel Metropole. He bumped into Bobby Charlton, Dennis Viollet and Frank Swift who were going out for a stroll, and since the night was quite mild, no one had a coat on, so Tommy gave Bobby his so he wouldn't catch a cold and, then he went off to bed.

The following events are told through the eyes of Albert Scanlon who, with a great deal of sadness talks about an accident that has lived forever in his memory.

"Everybody was glad when the final whistle went, it was a rough game and I'm sure the referee was born in Belgrade. If you spat on the floor you had a free kick given against you. Whenever you played in these Communist Countries it always seemed the first dozen rows were soldiers, but I'm sure it wasn't the soldiers who were throwing lumps of ice at us at the end. Bert and Tom hurried us into the dressing room and I'll always remember Matt's first words were 'well that's another one out of the way, we're there again'. He was elated and although it was a hard game we weren't tired, you see when you've just won a game like that the adrenalin was still flowing, the tiredness came the morning after.

After the presentation at the British Embassy me and Bill Foulkes went into this club which was nothing more than a cellar with a few tables scattered around. In the club was Tommy's friend, Sekularac, who was a bit of a gipsy, but a bloody good player. He was frightened to death of Duncan but he idolised Tommy, and with Tommy being the type of bloke he was, he went out for a drink with him after the Banquet. Anyhow he told us he had just left, but me and Bill didn't fancy this place so we went back to the hotel.

On the Thursday morning we all had breakfast and said all our farewells to the hotel staff and we got onto the coach to Zenum airport. Everything went well until we got to Munich. After coffee and sandwiches we boarded the plane, took our seats and made our way down the runway. There was quite a lot of snow about but it didn't worry me. As we went down the engines died, so we taxied back up the runway to get ready for a second go. As we set off again the same thing happened. We were all told to get off and make our way back into the lounge. We'd only been in there a couple of minutes when a voice came over the loudspeakers telling us to get back on board.

I was walking up the steps behind Frank Taylor, who said 'sod this, if you don't take off first time in the R.A.F. you scrap it'. It made no odds to me, I just did what I was told. As we got in I sat down with Bill and started playing cards. Bobby and Dennis had to come to the front and swapped places with Tommy and David who were now at the back because they thought it would be safer. The boss, Tosher, Bert and Walter were sat behind me. Meanwhile Mark was at the back because he never played cards and Eddie, who originally was at the front, moved to the rear as soon as Tommy and David did.

"As we started that third take-off I looked around and noticed Tommy wasn't in his seat and as I turned to the front the steward came running out and strapped himself into his seat, that wasn't very reassuring. Someone told me later that Tommy and David Pegg were in the toilets at the back of the plane. I remember going down the runway and then everything just went blank and as you know the tail end came away and burst into flames.

The next thing I remember is waking up with a pain in my head. Turning my head I looked straight at Dennis who looked at me and said 'Hello so you're awake then'. I was in the same room as Dennis Viollet, Ray Wood, Kenny Morgans and the Pilot. I had seen Duncan and Johnny in another room and I was told Matt, Frank Taylor and Jackie were in a room upstairs. So at first you just assume the others were slightly more injured than yourself, but in another part of the hospital. No one would tell me at first who had died, so in the end I asked a priest called Father O'Hagen to tell me the truth. It was the worst moment of my life when I was told about the lads dying".

Bill Foulkes (left), and Harry Gregg inspect the wreckage of the plane.

"Bert Whalley and Tosher Curry were the biggest loss for me, the others I was on a level with, but Tom was the first person who ever spoke to me when I went to Old Trafford as a kid. Bert was a calmer version of Jimmy. They were like a double act. Jimmy the firebrand who I was frightened to death of, but he was a tremendous fellow. Bert wasn't like that he was a gentleman who would do anything for you."

The Munich air disaster shocked the world. The plane had crashed into a house, which caught fire, and then a few yards further on had hit a wooden hut which housed fuel. The right side of the rear section was ripped away and what was left of the aircraft slid along the ground on its belly spinning before coming to a screeching halt.

Around this once sleek silver aircraft lay the dazed, dead or injured. Of the 44 people on board, 23 lost their lives. Tommy was one of those 21 casualties.

In Belgrade nobody could believe it, huge crowds had gathered outside the radio stations and News Agencies, waiting for news. It was a great shock to the Red Star player Sekularac. He had struck up a great friendship with his rival over the two games, and had even invited Tommy to spend his holidays in the summer with him on the Adriatic Coast. In return Tommy had asked his friend to come to England in June or July, Sekularac who once said of Tommy *"I will never forget his naive and attractive smile"*, sent a letter of condolence to Tommy's Mum and Dad soon after the crash.

Meanwhile back in Manchester, large crowds had gathered around Old Trafford waiting for any news. The City was stunned into a numb silence as people wept openly in the streets, and the headline in the 6.00 p.m. evening edition of the Evening Chronicle read:

"UNITED AIR DISASTER, 28 KILLED"

Back home in Barnsley, Bill was about to start work at the pit when someone told him about the crash but it never sank in and he just carried on with his shift as usual. It was only when he was on his way home on the bus and he looked over someone's shoulder and read the paper, that it was brought home to him. His brother Alec recalled at the time. *"Everything just went blank, I drove straight home and to this day I don't know whether I ran over anybody or not, I was that dazed"*.

Tommy's sister Irene, along with other members of his family, heard the news on the radio and immediately made her way to St. Helens Avenue to be with Tommy's Mum and Dad. The family stayed up all night waiting for news as it still hadn't been confirmed if Tommy had been one of those who had died. Meanwhile, that evening, Harry England had collected his wages from the pit and along with Bill Taylor, Bob McCormick and Eric Hodgson went up by car to Old Trafford to see if they could find out any more news.

Finally the family received a telegram on Friday afternoon confirming that Tommy had indeed been killed. It was now that they really began to grieve. His parents had lost a son, the others had lost a brother, many had lost a good friend. Jackie Blanchflower when talking about Munich years later said: *"Tommy Taylor's death was the worst for me, I have never been able to make a friendship like that since"*. Football, both in England and across Europe, had been robbed of one of its great stars.

The coffins arrived back in Manchester from Munich at Ringway Airport on Monday 10th February. In a twelve mile journey from Ringway to Old Trafford, people came by car, bike, and motorcycle. Two hours before the cortege passed, cars were parked bumper to bumper in an almost unbroken line. It was estimated that 100,000 people saw the cortege. Along the route silent faces were everywhere many in tears.

At the end of the journey, the twelve coffins were placed almost eerily into the gymnasium at Old Trafford, for a night Manchester will never forget.

Ex-team mate and friend Doug Kelly has the unwanted distinction of not only playing with both Tommy and Mark Jones, but also having attended both funerals. He remembers that time with sadness: *"I went up on the Tuesday to collect Mark's coffin, it was a bad time. All the coffins were identical, big heavy ones with chrome handles at the side and when you lifted them they hurt your knuckles, and the lids were held down by eight screws which were sealed by a German wax stamp. I suppose it was to stop anybody tampering with them. I was a pall bearer at Mark's funeral and his wife June was just hysterical, and at Tommy's I have never seen so many flowers, there was even a wreath from Cary Grant. A year or so later someone bought me the book 'The Day a Team Died', and I sat there and wept. I'll never forget Mark and Tommy."*

Tommy's coffin was brought home on the Wednesday and put into the front room of his family home in St. Helens Avenue. On Thursday 13th February 1958, Thomas Taylor was finally laid to rest at Monk Breton Parish Church. As the funeral made its way from St. Helens Avenue to the church the streets were lined with bareheaded and silent mourners four deep, and they remembered that it was exactly a week ago to the hour that the ill-fated plane tried to take off from Munich. Many in the crowd wore red rosettes - the colour of both Barnsley and Manchester United - draped with black ribbon, and many wept. As the cortege passed his former school, Burton Road Juniors, eleven boys in red football kits stood in silence and paid tribute.

At Oakwell and at the Town Hall, flags were flown at half-mast, and at the church Barnsley players formed a guard of honour as the coffin, which was carried by friends, Harry England, Eric Hodgson, Keith Hibberd, Dennis Hirst, Bob McCormick and Bob Nicholls came past. The F.A. had offered to send some players from the League to do this but the family declined saying that his friends would act as the bearers.

In the church a short and simple service was conducted by the Rev. W.A. Jubb. The plate on the coffin was simply inscribed *"Tommy Taylor - died February 6th 1958"*, and at the graveside a bugler sounded the 'Last Post'.

The mourners included Joe Richards, who represented the Football League, as did Walter Winterbottom. From Manchester came directors Mr. W. Petherbridge and Louis Edwards, assistant secretary Les Olive, Joe Armstrong, Gordon Clayton, Sandy Busby and Don Gibson, plus hundreds more. Pupils at Tommy's former school Raley raised some money for a wreath, but they had so much money left over they bought a silver cup and named it 'The Tommy Taylor Cup' and it was awarded to the most promising local footballer of the year.

"I don't think Tommy was ever replaced after Munich, because the way United played changed," Albert Scanlon says *"They tried Bobby and Alex Dawson up front, but they reverted back to Dennis in the end. Old Trafford wasn't the same place after the crash. I went to the 1958 Cup Final but - and don't get me wrong, the lads that got there got there on merit along with the crowd - after the first half I walked out because I kept thinking of the lads who should have been there.*

31st October 1959. Manchester United Supporters Club, Central Branch,
visit Tommy's grave. A coach was laid on from Manchester.
Tommy's father can be seen to the left of the 3rd lady.

Those were the lads I grew up with from when I was a sixteen-year old. I think Tommy, Roger and Duncan would have been in the England side for some time and one or two of the other lads would have gotten in as well. Eddie would have worked his way into the side and it would have taken a very good player to shift him. Dennis would have got capped earlier than he did.

Now I know Jimmy Murphy idolised Duncan, but I think he had a lot of secret admiration for Tommy. You should have seen Matt's and Jimmy's faces when Tommy was up front knocking the goals in.

I must say, in the five years I knew him, it was never 'Tommy Taylor of Manchester United and England' but always 'Tommy Taylor from Barnsley'. He never changed. I'll always remember him as someone who did his job week-in week-out full of fun and very talented.

You can put Tommy Taylor among the best two buys United every made. Denis Law was the other, and at the time of Munich Tommy was the best centre-forward in the country".

The black cloud of tragedy seldom descends over the world of sport. For sport has always been a way of leisure, great entertainment and for some people escapism. So when the cloud does descend it shakes every man and woman with its sudden horror.

This was proved after the plane carrying the Manchester United team crashed whilst trying to take off from a Munich runway. Of the 44 passengers on board 23 were killed almost instantly.

Captain Roger Byrne, Eddie Colman, David Pegg, Geoff Bent, Mark Jones, Bill Whelan, Duncan Edwards and Tommy were amongst those 23, as well as club officials Walter Crickmer, Bert Whalley and Tom Curry.

The disaster had torn apart the England football team and it certainly lessened its chances of doing well in the World Cup in Sweden that year. It destroyed one of the greatest club sides this country has ever seen, but what do these things matter? The real tragedy was personal - and so personal that it carried its sombre effect into almost every household in the country. These players were great entertainers, so very talented, and oh so very young. They were the last people you could imagine dying.

The impact of the crash was greater than it would have been if a hundred unknowns had died on that plane. The sensation of eight top class footballers dying a cruel death brought home in an instant to the people in the street about the uncertainty of life and with that uncertainty comes a strange sense of relief and personal thanksgiving. For many people at the time there were additional feelings as they read the news. Feelings of admiration for the work of the doctors and nurses at the Rechts der Isar Hospital in Munich, and sorrow as they saw members of the Manchester United football team struggling against death in hospital wards.

The tragedy of Munich shocked the world just as the aircrash at Turin had in May 1949, which involved Italian champions Torino, but when the United accident happened the memory of Turin was somewhat blurred, or totally forgotten from peoples minds.

In a career that was tragically cut short by the Munich Air Crash Tommy Taylor had been denied, in such a cruel fashion, a normal lifespan in a game which he loved so much.

From becoming a first team regular with Barnsley, his career lasted barely six seasons. During those six seasons, however, he set the football world alight with his goalscoring feats. He scored 28 goals from 46 appearances for Barnsley, 128 goals in 189 games for United and 16 goals from 19 appearances for England - a great achievement.

He was fortunate enough to play alongside some of the greatest names of that era. At Oakwell there was Eddie McMorran, Johnny Kelly and Danny Blanchflower. Old Trafford brought him together with Johnny Carey, Duncan Edwards and Roger Byrne, and in the white shirt of England he played with legends such as Tom Finney, Nat Lofthouse, Stanley Matthews and Billy Wright, all great names from the golden age of British Football. It's fitting that Tommy Taylor played alongside all of them for he was an all time great.

Finally, former Secretary to the Barnsley Football Association, Len Squires, recalls a chat he had with Matt Busby. He had gone to Manchester shortly after Tommy had signed for United to watch Barnsley play Manchester United in the Youth Cup. In the Directors room after the game he asked Matt what he really thought of Tommy.

Matt's reply was to the effect that in his opinion, Tommy Taylor would make one of the best centre-forwards in the world. How true those sentiments became, for Tommy's play and personality have left an impression of indelible greatness on the game of football. We have rarely seen his equivalent since.

TOMMY TAYLOR
1932 - 1958

CONCLUSION

It's now nearly forty years since Tommy died, but he has never been forgotten in either Barnsley and Manchester. Places where people still talk about him with a great deal of affection.

At Old Trafford his name, along with his fellow team mates, is on a Memorial Plaque as a permanent reminder of the players that died at Munich, and back home in Barnsley in the Athersley Pub you can find a picture of Tommy hanging in the tap room. A quick visit into town to Chennells Bar will reveal an assortment of Barnsley and Manchester United memorabilia gracing the walls, including one of Tommy's International Badges. Meanwhile in the Town Hall they proudly display the Tommy Taylor Cup.

The family has had its fair share of heartaches through the years. His mother had cancer but in 1952, after a successful operation she was given the all clear by the doctors. However after the crash the cancer returned and she was to die three years later. It is said she never got over Tommy's death.

By 1958 his father, Charles, was working at a local firm of Asphalters, but a couple of weeks after the crash he had a fall and a combination of this and his deteriorating eyesight forced him to retire for good. After a spell of living alone he was no longer able to cope and went to live with his daughters, first Irene and then Alice. He spent his last days at a home in Monk Breton where he died in 1978, aged 80.

Going blind is something that ran in the family. Most of Tommy's aunts and uncles, apart from his uncle Tucker, lost their sight. Sadly Uncle Tucker died recently of cancer, leaving Elliot and Elizabeth as the only two still alive.

His sister, Irene, who married Jim Kossowicz in 1949, had three children, Stephen, Lynn and Danusia. Stephen inherited some of Tommy's looks and he proudly wears his famous uncle's ring. It was originally a gift to Tommy from his parents on his 21st birthday.

Brother Alec was always a bit of a loner. He was a long distance lorry driver who, despite having many girlfriends, never married. Unfortunately he liked to drink too much, a liking which eventually led to pneumonia, he died at the early age of 46, in 1975.

Tommy's other brother, Albert, married in 1949 to Eleanor, and they had three children. One of them, Peter, is now the proud owner of a Brazilian No.9 shirt which his uncle had swapped at Wembley in 1956. Albert died in August, 1992.

Tommy's eldest sister, Alice, married and had one daughter. In the 1960's she moved to Richmond, North Yorkshire. Now a widow she lives alone but has never felt the need to return to Barnsley.

Finally younger brother Bill married Audrey in 1957, and Tommy was best man. Whilst Bill was working at the pits they began building up a successful bakery business.

His sight has also deteriorated, whether Tommy would have suffered the same we shall never know. Bill's only child, Ian, has now inherited the cabinet which houses all of Tommy's caps, medals and trophies.

In April 1958, Tommy was due to be best man at Harry England's wedding, and at the insistence of Violet, Harry wore a pair of Tommy's shoes for the big day. Harry and his wife Irene still live in Richard Road today, a street he has lived in for over fifty years. He is now the proud owner of an England blazer that his friend once wore with pride back in the 1950's.

Tommy's sports car was given to Carol after the crash, although she eventually had to sell it because she was unable to drive. Carol became best friends with Duncan Edwards' fiancee, Molly Leach, and they went on holidays together well into the early 1960's. Carol married a dentist and moved south, but the marriage didn't last and she eventually returned to Manchester. After an accident in 1988, she slipped into a coma from which she never awoke.

What if Tommy had survived the crash? We know that he had spoken about opening a sports shop after he had finished playing. Whether or not he had any intentions of a career as a coach or maybe even in management we shall never know.

At the time of his death the soccer world lay at his feet. United were on course, as in the previous season, going for the treble. The third successive championship would have been difficult to obtain but not impossible. They faced A.C. Milan in the European Cup semi-finals, and providing they won that match the final against the mighty Real Madrid would have been a fascinating contest. It would appear unlikely that the pre-Munich Manchester United would have lost to Bolton Wanderers in the 1958 Cup Final.

England were tipped to, at least, reach the final of the World Cup in Sweden, and for Tommy as the resident No.9, this achievement would have gone on to enhance his reputation as one of the world's great forwards. It took him a while to establish himself in the England side but for many games he was asked to play out of position, although he still managed sixteen goals in nineteen appearances, nearly a goal a game, and at the time of his death he was well on course to beating Nat Lofthouse's record of 30 goals for his country.

Tommy was only on the losing side for England on two occasions, and the regular trio from United of Taylor, Byrne, plus Edwards, had scored 17 goals in the previous 12 games and had remained unbeaten by foreign opposition for three years. Needless to say England failed to do well in the 1958 World Cup and it took a long time to recover the loss. Providing he kept fit and played well he could have gone on to play for his country for a few more years, for Tommy had just turned 26 when he died. Nat Lofthouse was 34 years old when he played his final England game.

Tommy Taylor will always be remembered for his goalscoring feats, and currently he is at No.9 in United's all time top scorers. A Great achievement when you consider he only had four full seasons at Old Trafford.

> *His name will always be mentioned whenever people talk about the great footballers of the past, and there follows just a few of the tributes to the boy from Smithies, by some well known names from the world of football.*

"First of all, professionally speaking now after all these years - and that includes twenty odd years as a manager - apart from the time spent at Old Trafford and the games I played with Tommy, I can honestly say that he was the best striker I played with and the best of his kind at the time. Success never changed Tom, I remember him making his debut at Old Trafford and scoring two goals against Preston.

The nice thing about Tom was his down-to-earth Yorkshire attitude to life, he never changed, he did not let success go to his head, on the contrary he gave us so many laughs with his sense of humour I can almost hear him now.

In fact writing this has given me many happy thoughts about Tom, who was without doubt the finest striker of his kind all the time he was at Old Trafford. Memories are nice to look back on and none nicer than the big, funny, lovable man from Barnsley. Thank you for bringing back many happy memories."

IAN GREAVES

"I believe Tommy played in 19 full Internationals for England, scoring 16 goals. He was a centre forward in the traditional English mould - like Tommy Lawton. A six footer, good in the air, fleet of foot with the ability to shoot with either leg, and with good skill in ball control and passing. At the time of the Munich disaster he had established himself as an automatic choice for the No.9 jersey.

I recall his splendid performances in two outstanding games for England. The first at Wembley against Brazil in 1956 when England won 4-2 (despite missing two penalties) and Tommy scored two great goals. Then later in Berlin where much to the delight of the thousands of British soldiers in the Olympic Stadium we defeated West Germany - with most of the players who had won the World Cup in 1954 - by the margin of 3-1.

We had the feeling that England was building a strong and confident team to win the World Cup in Sweden in 1958 - but the Munich disaster took away the spine of the side with the sad deaths of Duncan Edwards, Roger Byrne and Tommy.

Tommy was a likeable chap, ever cheerful in spirit and as a footballer he had that constantly lively, positive and determined attitude to lend great thrust to a forward line. He was respected and admired by all his fellow players and had the potential to win many more International Caps."

SIR WALTER WINTERBOTTOM   C.B.E.

"Tommy Taylor was the player we needed to round off the team, to complete the picture, a big strong finisher.

We bought him from Barnsley for £29,999 in 1953, knocking off the odd pound so he wouldn't be labled a £30,000 player. Tommy was ideal, brilliant in the air, so good he would rank with the greats. Not only could he head for goal with great power, he could also turn in the air and head delicately to a man either behind or alongside him.

He was a great finisher with his feet and very unselfish. He wanted to score goals himself, naturally, everyone does, but he didn't really mind who scored them as long as they went in. He was just as happy making goals for others as scoring them himself."

The Late SIR MATT BUSBY

"I hope you have much success with your book on Tommy. I was very pleased when Matt Busby, later Sir Matt of course, signed him. After watching him play for Barnsley I was very impressed and felt he would be a great goalscorer with Manchester United. My prediction was correct and he went on to score 112 League goals from 1953 to 1958.

Actually Tommy and I only played together for a short time, as I left to manage Blackburn Rovers, but I remember him as a very talented player and a very likeable young man."

JOHNNY CAREY

"Although I only spent a year playing with Tommy it was a great year and very enjoyable. He was a nice lad, very happy, a typical Yorkshireman who spoke with a very broad accent. He was good friends at the club with David Pegg, Jackie Blanchflower and Mark Jones, they were great lads too. I remember when we had a day off Mark took us shooting to a farm in Macclesfield as he knew the farmer. Tommy and myself had never done any shooting before and I don't think we laughed so much before in all our lives, it was a great day.

As a player I think he would have got better as he got older and he would have certainly won more caps. He was always very fit but you could never call him a dirty player, he always played the ball. He was a great lad whom I liked very much."

HENRY COCKBURN

"Although I only played with Tommy on a few occasions, I played against him many times. To me he was a really great player. Both in the air and on the ground, everything was done with a minimum amount of fuss. When he went to head a ball he appeared to hang in the air and on the ground he was in complete control of the ball. As you know, Tommy came from Barnsley and I from Sheffield so we were both 'Yorkies'. I would have loved to have played with him many more times but it was not to be. Believe me they don't come any better than Tommy. Both as a footballer and as a man he was a fabulous person and it will be a long time before we see his kind again."

ALBERT QUIXALL

"Tommy Taylor and I worked together, in modern terminology we would be the two strikers. What a pleasure it was to play with him. He was the perfect foil for me. Many's the time he would fool the defenders into following him, letting the ball run on and leaving a clear path for me.

I remember him working down the flank, as in the Bilbao game, when he ran rings round Garay, probably the best centre-half in the world. Off he'd go with his big, beautiful, graceful movement, amazing in such a big bloke. He was wonderful to watch with all his power he really put defences under pressure. But whenever I think of Tom, I see him soaring two or three feet above a defender and his powerful back would arch and with perfect timing he would head the ball into the back of the net. A great player and a great person to be with."

DENNIS VIOLLET

"Tommy Taylor was an outstanding centre-forward in the great United side of the 50's and also for England, and had great qualities in his head and shooting ability. He was extremely quick and a clinical finisher. I played with him in the England side and it was obvious he had outstanding ability as a centre-forward and a prolific scorer of goals. I remember playing against him at Old Trafford with Preston and he had a great game, scoring two goals as they beat us 5-2.

It was a great tragedy that he and so many outstanding players were lost in the Munich air crash as I am convinced he would have gone on to be one of the all-time greats of English soccer."

TOM FINNEY

"Tommy was a great lad and very down to earth. One of the things that sticks out in my mind is that when the season was over Tommy loved to get back to Barnsley to be with his old pals and relax for a few weeks having a few pints. He used to put on a stone in weight in the close season and he had to work hard to get it off when we started training.

He used to ask Tom Curry if he had his boo-its ready for the new season. Boo-its being his football boots. We used to play cards a lot on trips away (three card brag) and whenever he won a few quid he was off to buy himself some new gear, so he wouldn't booze it. I think Tommy brought Jackie Blanchflower out of his shell because when you went out with him it was free and easy all the way. Jackie being the quiet type had to change to keep up with his pal. But at the time we were all close and they were a great bunch of lads."

RAY WOOD

"Well, what can I say about Tommy Taylor. I suppose my best memory of him was that he had great ability, was very mobile and had excellent ball control. He had great shooting strength and he would have got better as he was only 26 when he died. His great strength was always in the air, in fact he was a young Tommy Lawton and that's the highest praise anyone can give."

The late BILLY WRIGHT C.B.E.

"The pen of George Follows was stilled at the Munich Air Crash. But the phrase that George used to describe Tommy Taylor, lives on in my mind.

George used the phrase 'The Smiling Executioner' in one of his many dispatches as he travelled around Europe with Manchester United ... and it fitted perfectly, for Tommy took that smile around the pitches of England and the goals he scored were scored with the finality of an executioner.

Tommy also left a legacy for future players, because he was the first English player I saw, to raise his right hand to the terraces when he scored. And I think he 'borrowed' that signal from the great Alfredo di Stefano when United played in Madrid.

It was in Madrid also, that I was summoned to the telephone to answer a call for Mr. Taylor. I was met by a deep-throated seductive voice informing me the lady was one of Spain's most famous flamenco dancers and that she had called to wish the smiling Mr. Taylor good success against Real Madrid.

*I had to interrupt, to tell the lady the gentleman she wished to speak to was the smiling and handsome **Tommy Taylor** .... and I would call him to the telephone immediately .... which I did.*

Tommy was a charmer, but his real value as a player was perhaps best recognised by the elite group of players who played with or against him. For example I was in Manchester's Queen's Hotel one evening with a group of Arsenal players who challenged me: 'Who is the best English centre-forward?'

I suggested Tom Finney, but I was quickly silenced: 'No the big fella down the road... if you watch him closely you will find that most teams like us, have two men covering him in the penalty area. Especially when the ball is in the air ... like John Charles, he's lethal.' "

FRANK TAYLOR O.B.E.

TOMMY TAYLOR

Born: 4 Quarry Street, Smithies.   29th January 1932.
Died: Munich Germany   6th February 1958

CAREER DETAILS

Barnsley Boys and Raley Secondary Modern School: 1944-46
Smithies United: 1948

- BARNSLEY F.C. -

Signed: (Amateur) 7th February 1948.   (Professional) 25th July 1949
First team debut: 2nd May 1950 v. St.Mirren (Paisley Charity Cup)
Football League debut: 7th October 1950 v. Grimsby Town (Division 2)
First F.A.Cup game: 10th January 1953 v. Brighton & H.A. (3rd round)
Last League game: 14th February 1953 v. Lincoln City (Division 2)

(Football League)	Appearances	Goals
1950/51	12	7
1951/52	4	0
1952/53	28	19
F.A.Cup	2	2
Total:	46	28

- MANCHESTER UNITED F.C. -

Signed: 4th March 1953
Football League debut: 7th March 1953 v. Preston North End (Division 1)
First F.A.Cup game: 9th January 1954 v. Burnley (3rd round)
European Cup debut: 12th September 1956 v. Anderlecht (1st round)

(Football League)	Appearances	Goals
1952/53	11	7
1953/54	35	22
1954/55	30	20
1955/56	33	25
1956/57	32	22
1957/58	25	16
F.A.Cup	9	5
European Cup	14	11
Total:	189	128

Appearances For England (goals in brackets)

Full Internationals:
1953:   v. Argentina, Chile (1), Uruguay (1).
1954:   v. Belgium, Switzerland.
1956:   v. Scotland, Brazil (2), Sweden, Finland, West Germany, Northern Ireland,
           Yugoslavia (2)(sub.), Denmark (3).
1957   v. Republic of Ireland (3), Denmark (2), Republic of Ireland, Wales, Northern Ireland,
           France (2)
Total: 19 games, 16 goals.
England 'B':
1956   v. Scotland (1), v. Switzerland (3) - 2 games, 4 goals.

Grand Total: 253 appearances   176 goals.
(Also represented The British Army, The Football Association, and The Football League)

A SELECTION OF TITLES

From
'YORE PUBLICATIONS'
12 The Furrows, Harefield,
Middx. UB9 6AT

(Free lists issued 3 times per year. For your first list please send a S.A.E.)

DONNY - The Official History of Doncaster Rovers *(Tony Bluff and Barry Watson)* Written by two supporters of the Club, with the full statistics (from 1879) incl. line-ups (from 1901). The book is well illustrated, with the full written history of the Club. Hardback with dustjacket and 240 pages. Price £14-95 plus £1-80 postage.

COLCHESTER UNITED - The Official History of the 'U's' *(Hal Mason)* With football involvement from the 1920's, the Author - a former journalist and Colchester programme editor - is well qualified to relate this complete history of the Club since its formation in 1937 (including complete statistics and lineups from this season). Large Hardback with dustjacket, 240 pages, priced £14-95 plus £2-70 postage.

AMBER IN THE BLOOD - History of Newport County: *(Tony Ambrosen).* The full written story of football in Newport from the pre-County days up to and including the recently formed Newport AFC club. The text is well illustrated, and a comprehensive statistical section provides all the results, attendances, goalscorers, etc. from 1912 to 1993 - the various Leagues and principal Cup competitions; additionally seasonal total players' appearances are included. A hardback book, containing 176 large pages is exceptional value at only £13-95 plus £2-60 postage.

KILLIE - The Official History (125 Years of Kilmarnock F.C.) *(David Ross).* A very detailed history of Scotland's oldest professional Club. The statistics section (including line-ups) cover the period 1873 to 1994, and over 200 illustrations, incl.a team group for most seasons. A large hardback of 256 pages, priced £15-95 plus £3-50 postage.

REJECTED F.C. VOLUME 1 (Reprint) *(By Dave Twydell)* The revised edition of this popular book - now in hardback - this volume provides the comprehensive histories of: Aberdare Athletic, Ashington, Bootle, Bradford (Park Avenue), Burton (Swifts, Wanderers and United), Gateshead/South Shields, Glossop, Loughborough, Nelson, Stalybridge Celtic and Workington. The 288 well illustrated pages also contain the basic statistical details of each club. Price £12-95 plus £1-30 postage. (Also *Rejected F.C. of Scotland:* Volume 1 covers Edinburgh and The South (Edinburgh City, Leith Athletic, St.Bernards, Armadale, Broxburn United, Bathgate, Peebles Rovers, Mid-Annandale, Nithsdale Wanderers and Solway Star - 288 pages). Volume 2 covers Glasgow and District (Abercorn, Arthurlie, Beith, Cambuslang, Clydebank, Cowlairs, Johnstone, Linthouse, Northern, Third Lanark, and Thistle - 240 pages). Each priced £12-95 plus £1-30 postage.

FOOTBALL LEAGUE - GROUNDS FOR A CHANGE (By Dave Twydell). A 424 page, A5 sized, Hardback book. A comprehensive study of all the Grounds on which the current English Football League clubs previously played. Every Club that has moved Grounds is included, with a 'Potted' history of each, plus 250 illustrations. Plenty of 'reading' material, as well as an interesting reference book. Price £13-95 Plus £1-70 Postage.

THROUGH THE TURNSTILES *(by Brian Tabner)* This incredible book which provides the average attendance of every English Football League club, for every season from 1888/89 to 1991/92. Well illustrated, and also relates the development of the game (angled towards attendances). Also details of the best supported 'away' teams, season ticket sales over the years, etc. A large format hardback and 208 packed pages. An excellent read at £13-95 plus £1-70 Postage.

COVENTRY CITY FOOTBALLERS (The Complete Who's Who)
By Martin & Paul O'Connor. One of the most detailed books of its type. Every Football (and Southern) League player has been included - around 700. Seasonal appearances of every player, brief personal details, 'pen pictures', together with very detailed information on the movements of the players to other clubs. Plus: around 100 photo's of the Club's most memorable men, and information on the principal players from the very early days. A hardback book with 224 large pages. £13-95 plus £2-60 postage.

HISTORY OF THE LANCASHIRE FOOTBALL ASSOCIATION 1878-1928. A rare historical and fascinating hardback reprint (first published in 1928). Contains the history of the formative days of Lancashire football. Sections within the 288 pages include the early histories of about 20 Clubs (**Manchester Utd.**, Wigan Borough, Rochdale, etc.), Lancashire Cup competitions, Biographies, etc. For those interested in the development of the game, this is a 'must', and you will definitely not be disappointed. Price £12-95 Plus £1-30 Postage.

THE CODE WAR *(Graham Williams)*
A fascinating look back on football's history - from the earliest days up to the First World War. 'Football' is covered in the broadest sense, for the book delves into the splits over the period to and from Rugby Union and Rugby League, as well as Football (Soccer). Potted histories of many of the Clubs are included, as is a comprehensive index. 192 page hardback, price £10-95 plus £1-20 postage.

84